The beginning of this boo taught in my church which made a great impact on congregation. Our church then encouraged Jim Richards to put it in book form and share it with others. What you have in your hands is the outcome of that work; I know you will be blessed.
Dr. Troy Brooks, Senior Pastor
First Baptist Church, Madisonville, TX

This book on Revelation really means so much to me. It makes extremely clear the pretribulation rapture of the church and the premillennial return of Christ and answers many questions about the end times, what happens to the church, and when the church is raptured. The timing of the great tribulation, the return of Christ to reign on the earth for a thousand years, and the establishment of the eternal kingdom of God, in which we who have trusted Jesus will live with Him, is explained in Chapters 21 and 22. I especially enjoyed reading this book because it reflects precisely Dr. W. A. Criswell's theology which he preached faithfully for over fifty years in our First Baptist Church of Dallas. I think this book will be a great help to all Christians and especially to Christians who have recently given their hearts and souls and destinies to the Lord Jesus.
Jack Pogue, Chairman
W. A. Criswell Foundation

Perhaps there is no book in the Bible as ignored in our day as is the last one – The Revelation. Can you imagine following a novel through its twists and turns and then putting it down before reading the last chapter? Yet that is what many believers do with the Bible. Dr. Jim Richards brings focus on this last book of the Bible with clarity and conviction. After all, God promises a special blessing upon those who "HEAR and HEED" what is written in the Revelation "for the time is near" (Revelation 1:3). Yes, *The Best is Yet to Come*. Read it and reap!
Dr. O. S. Hawkins, President/CEO
GuideStone Financial Resources

Many people are intimidated by the book of Revelation because they think it is too complicated. Dr. Richards removes that obstacle with this straightforward guide to the biblical text from the pretribulation/premillennial point of view. He also reminds us that there is a promised blessing for those who read, hear, and do what is contained in this New Testament book. Don't miss out on the blessing. Study Revelation and understand *The Best is Yet to Come.*

Dr. Jerry A. Johnson, President & CEO
National Religious Broadcasters

Often works on "last things" are too complicated. Readers and students get lost in a maze of inscrutable details. Dr. Richards' work on the Lord's return avoids that. Our national pastors and workers in South Asia begged for an English transcript of his book, because they understood it. I join them! If you want clear, Bible explanations of Revelation, here it is.

Dr. David H. Shepherd, TSL, South Asia
International Mission Board, SBC

Revelation

Revelation

The Best is Yet to Come

Jim Richards

ANEKO Press

www.lifesentencepublishing.com

Revelation: The Best is Yet to Come – Jim Richards and Frank Ball

Copyright © 2014

Scripture taken from the New King James Version®. Copyright © 1982 by Thomas Nelson, Inc. Used by permission.

Printed in the United States of America

First edition published 2014

LIFE SENTENCE Publishing books are available at discounted prices for ministries and other outreach. Find out more by contacting us at info@lspbooks.com

ANEKO Press, LIFE SENTENCE Publishing, and its logo are trademarks of

LIFE SENTENCE Publishing, LLC
P.O. Box 652
Abbotsford, WI 54405

Paperback ISBN: 978-1-62245-180-7

Ebook ISBN: 978-1-62245-181-4

10 9 8 7 6 5 4 3 2 1

This book is available from www.amazon.com, Barnes & Noble, and your local bookstore.

Cover Design: Amber Burger

Illustrations: Allen Sutton

Editor: Sheila Wilkinson

Dedication

*God's serendipitous gifts to my wife, June, and me
are our three precious grandchildren. Hannah,
Julia, and Harrison do not face an uncertain future.
They are sure to be blessed as they put their trust in
the Lord Jesus. Great is His faithfulness!*

Contents

Foreword

A pastor sits before his open Bible on Saturday evening, turning the pages lackadaisically and hoping that something will leap from the pages and suggest itself to him as a sermon topic for Sunday morning. He has been thinking about it all week, but no text has come to his mind. Furthermore, he is concerned that what may interest him may utterly fail to stir the hearts of his listeners in the morning. What is this pastor to do now?

Jim Richards, Executive Director of the Southern Baptists of Texas Convention, has an idea that will stir your soul and invigorate the entire congregation. This poignant volume that you hold in your hand is the key to your future preaching. Richards knows several salient truths that are so obvious that most miss them. First, what the people want to hear is the Word of God. They will tolerate topical sermons because they have been taught to do so, but what their spirits relish is a text-driven sermon that explains what God thinks about any subject.

Second, Richards also knows that walking through a book of the Bible from the first verse to the last is the best way to grasp what the author's intention was and the finest conceivable way to develop a well-grounded theology based on the Word of God. Finally, Richards knows that curiosity about the Apocalypse is such that announcing a series of sermons on this book will usually increase attendance by at least 10 percent in any congregation. Furthermore, the author well grasps the fact that to do a six-volume commentary on a book of the Bible is not necessary to make it come to life in the heart of the preacher and in the lives of his auditors.

This little volume on Revelation takes the reader on a journey that captures the essence of each chapter and adds important addenda to the conclusion of the book. Richards' grasp of the central theme of each chapter as a guide of the interpretation of the whole not only enlightens the eyes but also challenges the heart to acquiescence at the hearing of the Word of God.

Jim Richards' assessment of the messages to the seven churches embraces the fact that there is a universality to the messages. Certainly they spoke to the actual historical churches of the time, but these thoughts serve to illumine the conditions and circumstances of churches today. As such, Richards finds marvelous insights into churchmanship even as he interprets the letters to these seven churches in Asia.

Beginning with chapter 4 and following, Richards outlines the course of the future based on the prophetic insights of John and bolstered by supporting passages from elsewhere in Holy Scripture. The outline that he provides for those events is a demonstration that history is not pinging off the walls of eternity in a breakaway, uncontrolled sprint. Quite to the contrary and much different from the feel of someone living in the 21st century, God's masterful control over events hastens to move us toward the eschaton and the triumph of Christ and the enthronement of good. In the understanding of the nature of the events of the last days and the consummation of the age, Richards finds again the rich providences of God, which make the worship of the Lord a delight.

Arriving at the end of the book of Revelation, Richards is

determined to capture something of the glory of God and the fullness of His provision for those who love Him. That occurs in the chapters on heaven. If, however, you struggle with comprehension of the heavenly revelation, you are nevertheless introduced by Richards' insights to the central truth that heaven is not at all like most evangelicals have imagined but infinitely more than anything you can get your arms around here on earth. The supremacy of Christ and the plan of God come together in a unique and remarkable way.

Pastor, if you are wondering what to preach, try the book of Revelation and take Jim Richards' handbook as the first guide to the book. Once you have decided on your text and marinated it thoroughly in prayer, read Jim Richards' *Revelation* and then turn to the more extensive commentaries. You will be able to go to them with assurance and understanding.

For the layman who simply wishes to get a quick feel for what the Apocalypse is all about, you could not have found a more helpful treatment than this one. The simple reading of this book will put you in a position to grasp the infinite vistas of John's marvelous presentation of last day events. Whether layman or preacher, this volume on Revelation is for you.

Paige Patterson, President
Southwestern Baptist Theological Seminary
Fort Worth, Texas

Acknowledgements

M any people have been contributors to this book. To a certain degree this book is a sum total of the influences on my life. My first pastor, Joe Mongle, preached the second coming of our Lord Jesus. Professors like Corbett Mask taught the imminent return of Christ. Church members like Jack and Elsie Adcock paid my way to Israel when I was a young preacher. The trip solidified my conviction that God was not through with Israel.

Of course the actual composition of the work involved specific individuals. Kenneth Priest has been the most invaluable of all. His recommendations always lead me down the right path toward publication. Frank Ball provided content editing to make the material much more readable. Judy Van Hooser transcribed messages, cleaning up grammatical errors. She later provided an eye for proper punctuation.

This book had its origin with a suggestion from Pastor Troy Brooks. After a series of lessons at First Baptist Church, Madisonville, Texas, Troy insisted that I put the material in book form. Troy asked for the church's affirmation. They agreed to buy copies as soon as it was published. An anonymous donor in the church provided funds for the publication. It all came together under the direction of the Spirit.

I am grateful for leaders like Paige Patterson and O. S. Hawkins who are willing to place their stamp of approval on such an elementary work. I am thankful for peers like Jerry Johnson and David Shepherd who took the time to write endorsements.

My duties at the Southern Baptists of Texas Convention are twenty-four seven. Yet I was able to do this work during my rest time away from the office. My co-laborers at the SBTC have been an encouragement, especially Randi Kent, my personal assistant.

My dear wife, June, endured more of my time away as I had to concentrate on writing. She is my greatest ministry partner. Finally, I know it is God's good pleasure to allow me to have this final product to provide for His glory. The good that comes from this book is all to the glory of God.

I pray you will find inspiration and challenge as your read the Revelation of Jesus Christ. May we begin every day with the prayer, "Even so, come Lord Jesus!"

Introduction

When Jesus said, "Repent and believe the Gospel," He was giving us the two components of appropriating the forgiveness of sin and eternal life. "For God so loved the world that He gave His only begotten Son, that whoever believes in Him should not perish but have everlasting life" (John 3:16). So that means, when you have Jesus, you have everlasting life. You can't ever be lost again.

That's the Gospel. That's how you're saved. If you know Jesus as your personal Lord and Savior, here's what's going to happen to you when He comes in the clouds.

Paul the apostle wrote, "For the Lord Himself will descend from heaven with a shout, with the voice of an archangel, and with the trumpet of God. And the dead in Christ will rise first. Then we who are alive and remain shall be caught up together with them in clouds to meet the Lord in the air" (1 Thessalonians 4:16, 17). Those who are taken will be the righteous saints who are caught away to meet Him in the clouds.

Jesus could come at any moment. It's a sweet promise to those who know Him.

Saved people will be caught away before the tribulation takes place. World conditions are dangerous now, but it's going to get worse. The rampant violence today is only a precursor of what it will be like after the rapture.

God gave the *Revelation of Jesus Christ* to show His servants what must shortly take place. Here's what you can expect if you're among those who are taken.

The best is yet to come!

Section I

The Past

Chapter 1

Revelation Chapter 1 begins our journey, just as climbing a few steps to the porch that takes us to the door that opens into the house of breathtaking insight. John the apostle has invited us to join him in his walk in the Spirit through time, viewing images which reveal the past, present, and future.

Let's open the door with these verses:

> ¹ The Revelation of Jesus Christ, which God gave Him to show His servants – things which must shortly take place. And He sent and signified it by His angel to His servant John, ² who bore witness to the word of God, and to the testimony of Jesus Christ, to all things that he saw. ³ Blessed is he who reads and those who hear the words of this prophecy, and keep those things which are written in it; for the time is near.

So here we have it – a promised blessing to those of us who read the book, understand the message, and say yes to what God is calling us to do. The word *revelation* comes from the Greek word *apocalypse*, which means "taking away the veil."

As we read and carefully consider His Word, we discover the truth that has been hidden from our eyes.

This revelation was given to Jesus by the Father. In His humanity, Jesus had restricted Himself from knowing everything. Some details about end-time events were known only by the Father. In His humanity, Jesus could not tell people everything they wanted to know about the last days.

When the disciples asked when the end time would come, Jesus said, "But of that day and hour no one knows, not even the angels of heaven, but My Father only" (Matthew 24:36). The information Jesus gave the disciples was not a result of something He had studied. The time and circumstances of His return were a revelation from His Father in Heaven.

We read in Revelation 22:10 that the time is near, and the words of prophecy in this book should not remain a secret.

Some people oppose the study of the book of Revelation, saying we cannot possibly understand what it means, that we would be wasting our time. They are right that it contains mysteries we may never understand, but we should not let that fact keep us from what God wants to show us today. We read in Revelation 22:10 that the time is near, and the words of prophecy in this book should not remain a secret. It is a book we should study. We should seek to know all God will speak to our hearts.

Do we really need the book of Revelation in our Bibles? Some people think preaching the Gospel is all we need today. Certainly, the Gospel is important, but the apostle Paul says we should preach "the whole counsel of God" (Acts 20:27), which is all of God's Word from Genesis to Revelation. Specific to the vision, we see this exhortation eight times in the book of Revelation: "He who has an ear, let him hear what the Spirit says."

Some scholars say the mysterious images and symbols were kind of Morse code that only first-century Christians were meant to understand. Peter would not agree with that view, and we shouldn't either. He says, "No prophecy of Scripture is of any private interpretation" (2 Peter 1:20). The prophetic Word is for public consumption, open for believers around the world to read and understand.

Others have said, "Well, I just don't think prophecy is worth studying. That stuff is off in the future somewhere. It hasn't happened for two thousand years. It may be another two thousand years. It's not going to happen in my lifetime, so I don't need to be concerned about it." Be careful with that reasoning, because Jesus said people would think that way right up until the day of their destruction. Just like it was in the days of Noah, people will be partying and pursuing pleasures, unconcerned about predictions of a worldwide calamity (Luke 17:26–27).

The apostle Paul said, "Be diligent to present yourselves approved to God, a worker who does not need to be ashamed, rightly dividing the word of truth" (2 Timothy 2:15). In this same letter to Timothy, he wrote, "All Scripture is given by inspiration of God, and is profitable for doctrine, for reproof, for correction, for instruction in righteousness, that the man of God may be complete, thoroughly equipped for every good work" (2 Timothy 3:16–17).

The book of Revelation is inspired from God, hand delivered from the Father to the Son, and from the Son – the Lord Jesus Christ – to John, the one who wrote the book to reveal this information to us. Today these words come by the Holy Spirit to inspire us and give us life.

Some theologians who like to categorize Scripture hold different views about the book of Revelation.

The Preterist view says all the book of Revelation is history – simply an allegorical writing about historical events that have already taken place. Others believe the book is historical in the sense that its fulfillment has been progressing from the first century through today.

Some view the book as both historical and spiritual. That is, the events that happened long ago have a spiritual application for us today. By understanding our past, we are better equipped to handle the future. Certainly, there is some truth to that view. We do well to learn from our mistakes.

The fourth position is common among those who may identify themselves as "premillennial," "pretribulation," or "futurists," a view that is most worthy of our consideration in looking at this book. We see the book of Revelation containing prophecy, a description of conditions people will experience in coming years.

The blessing belongs to us if we'll study the book. We can be exceptions to what Jesus said most people will be doing – eating and drinking, partying and pursuing pleasures, either unaware or not caring what lies ahead. Unlike them, we can be prepared.

In Chapter 1 verses 4–20, we have the introduction to the vision John received. Let's look at verses 4–6.

[4] John, to the seven churches which are in Asia:

Grace to you and peace from Him who is and who was and who is to come, and from the seven Spirits who are before His throne, [5] and from Jesus Christ, the faithful witness, the firstborn from the dead, and the ruler over the kings of the earth.

To Him who loved us and washed us from our sins in His own blood, [6] and has made us kings and priests to His God and Father, to Him be glory and dominion forever and ever. Amen.

Here we have the setting of the scene. John is letting the people of the seven churches know he is writing Holy Scripture from God to them. Those churches were located in the country that now is called Turkey, with Russia and Ukraine to the north, and Syria, Israel, and Saudi Arabia to the south. If you travel to Turkey, you can see the archeological sites where those churches are believed to be located.

Besides speaking to the 7 churches of Asia, the book of Revelation refers to many other "7s." There are 7 churches, 7 seals, 7 trumpets, 7 personages, 7 vials, 7 dooms, and 7 new things – even 7 spirits of the Lord. Those seven spirits are named by the prophet Isaiah, which would make an interesting study (Isaiah 11:2).

In biblical numerology, the number 7 speaks of completeness. The book of Revelation tells us about the end times and is the *completion* of God's revelation.

As prophet, priest, and king, Jesus fulfills all the Old Testament offices of ministry.

In verses 7 and 8, we find the introduction to the second coming of Jesus.

> [7] Behold, He is coming with clouds, and every eye will see Him, even they who pierced Him. And all the tribes of the earth will mourn because of Him. Even so, Amen.

> [8] "I am the Alpha and the Omega, the Beginning and the End," says the Lord, "who is and who was and who is to come, the Almighty."

These words fulfill what was foretold by prophets of old: "And I will pour on the house of David and on the inhabitants of Jerusalem the Spirit of grace and supplication; then they will look on Me whom they pierced. Yes, they will mourn for Him as one mourns for his only son, and grieve for Him as one grieves for a firstborn" (Zechariah 12:10).

A day will come when every eye will behold Him. Those who pierced Him will see Him. Jesus – the Alpha and Omega, the beginning and the end. He is the A to Z. He is all we need.

> *A day will come when every eye will behold Him.*

In verses 9–18, the Sovereign Savior is introduced. We actually get a snapshot of Jesus, which everybody can see like a photo posted on Facebook.

> [9] I, John, both your brother and companion in the tribulation and kingdom and patience of Jesus Christ, was on the island that is called Patmos for the word of God and for the testimony of Jesus Christ. [10] I was in the Spirit on the Lord's Day, and I heard behind me a loud voice, as of a trumpet, [11] saying, "I am the Alpha and the Omega, the First and the Last," and, "What you see, write in a book and send it to the seven churches which are in Asia: to Ephesus, to Smyrna, to Pergamos, to Thyatira, to Sardis, to Philadelphia, and to Laodicea."

> [12] Then I turned to see the voice that spoke with me. And having turned I saw seven golden lampstands, [13] and in the midst of the seven lampstands One like the Son of Man, clothed with a garment down to the feet and girded about the chest with a golden band. [14] His head and hair were white like wool, as white as snow, and His eyes like a flame of fire; [15] His feet were like fine brass, as if refined in a furnace, and His voice as the sound of many waters; [16] He had in

His right hand seven stars, out of His mouth went a sharp two-edged sword, and His countenance was like the sun shining in its strength. [17] And when I saw Him, I fell at His feet as dead. But He laid His right hand on me, saying to me, "Do not be afraid; I am the First and the Last. [18] I am He who lives, and was dead, and behold, I am alive forevermore. Amen. And I have the keys of Hades and of Death.

Earlier, John was the pastor of the church at Ephesus until times when Christians were severely persecuted. Because of his testimony for the Lord Jesus, the Roman government sent John into exile, banishing him to the isle of Patmos in the Aegean Sea, about thirty miles off the western coast of Turkey. While on this island, isolated from people, he came into the presence of the Lord through this vision.

He says this event happened on "the Lord's Day." Which day was that?

Sometimes we think of the past in terms defined by familiar conditions in the present. For most of us today, we think of the Lord's Day as Sunday, our most common day of worship. Perhaps that is what he meant.

On the other hand, I believe it's more likely that John was transported in his vision to the last day to be able to see the end time. He was taken to "the Day of days," the last of days, a time when the history of nations is brought to a close, a time when the Lord returns, which is known as "the Lord's Day."

Old Testament prophets looked to the time when the Messiah would come as the "day of the Lord" (Malachi 4:5). The apostle Peter refers to the "day of the Lord" when Jesus will return, "in which the heavens will pass away with a great noise, and the elements will melt with fervent heat; both the earth and the works that are in it will be burned up" (2 Peter 3:10).

John receives this message from Jesus for the churches of Asia, but these words are applicable for churches everywhere and for all time.

In the vision, Jesus appears in high-priestly attire. Remember, Jesus filled three offices of the Old Testament.

Truly, He was a prophet, revealing the heart and mind of the Father, revealing conditions known only by God, and accurately predicting His death, burial, and resurrection, as well as events which took place shortly after His ascension to Heaven. He prophesied conditions and events far into the future, even to the last days.

Jesus is our coming King, and the book of Revelation has much to say about His position of kingship.

He is also our High Priest, standing by the Father, interceding on our behalf, just as the deacon Stephen saw while being stoned, saying, "Look! I see the heavens opened and the Son of Man standing at the right hand of God!" (Acts 7:56). Jesus stands there today, ministering for us.

The Bible says, "There is one God and one Mediator between God and men, the Man Christ Jesus" (1 Timothy 2:5). In Old Testament worship, the high priest would go into the Holy of Holies to worship God, interceding for the people and offering a blood sacrifice for people's sins. In the same manner, Jesus entered Heaven's most holy place and offered His own blood that our sins might be forgiven, acting as our High Priest. Yes, even today, Jesus is our Savior, Mediator, and Intercessor – our High Priest.

John says in his letters to Christians, "My little children, these things I write to you, so that you may not sin. And if anyone sins, we have an *Advocate* with the Father, Jesus Christ the righteous" (1 John 2:1, emphasis added).

Instead of High Priest, which was a perfect image for people in the first century, perhaps we can better understand His role if we think of Him as our attorney, the One who defends us for the sins we have committed. He is the One who intercedes for us in Heaven's court, arguing on our behalf, saying we are forgiven. We should not be punished. In the description of Jesus, we see the likeness of God Himself. Look back at His physical appearance, beginning in verse 14.

> *It's a picture of our Lord Jesus Christ, who is the same, yesterday, today, and forever*

- His hair represents wisdom.
- His eyes are omniscient. He knows and sees all things.
- His feet, as brass, are a symbol of judgment.
- His voice, like many waters, speaks of supreme authority, perhaps like the deafening roar we hear at Niagara Falls, except with a clear, unmistakable message.
- His countenance is the Shekinah glory of God.
- He calms our fears.
- He brings us life.
- He is the living Lord, resurrected from the grave, ascended to Heaven, and now at the right hand of the Father.
- He is the coming Lord as He will appear one day.

This is what John saw and what he wants us all to see, which is more than a casual Facebook photo from the past. It's a picture of our Lord Jesus Christ, who is the same, yesterday, today, and forever (Hebrews 13:8) – eternal and unchanging.

Let's look at the next two verses.

¹⁹ "Write the things which you have seen, and the

things which are, and the things which will take place after this. [20] The mystery of the seven stars which you saw in My right hand, and the seven golden lampstands: The seven stars are the angels of the seven churches, and the seven lampstands which you saw are the seven churches."

Here, we find the organizational key to the book of Revelation, which might be worth marking in your Bible. John is told to (1) "write the things which you have seen," (2) "the things which are," and (3) "the things which will take place after this." Now we know the sequence in which the book will be divided. Section I is the past – Chapter 1. Section II is the present – Chapters 2 and 3. Section III is the future – Chapters 4–22.

Our best approach is to let truth explain truth.

Back in verse 20, we're shown how we should interpret some of the book's symbols. Without this clarification, our minds would be left to imagine all kinds of possibilities, leaving us in a state of confusion, unsure of what to believe. Of course, we don't have all the answers. On earth, our understanding will always be limited to the details that God chooses to reveal.

Sometimes, scholars think they need to come across as knowing everything. They have studied long and hard and want you to know they have figured everything out. They take their theories and present them as fact, which I believe is not pleasing the Lord. I'm not sure what God thinks of them – maybe something like a cross between a skunk and a computer – a stinking know-it-all.

Our best approach is to let truth explain truth. The apostle Paul says, "All Scripture is given by inspiration of God, and is profitable for doctrine, for reproof, for correction, for instruction in righteousness" (2 Timothy 3:16). Therefore, we can look at other Bible verses to better understand the abundant symbolism in the book of Revelation. There is no doubt that God has left some of the details yet to be filled in. But we should not let the mystery prevent us from seeing the message that God has made plain through Scripture. If you look back at verses 12 and 13, you will see 7 golden lampstands and Jesus standing in the midst. In verse 16, Jesus has the 7 stars in His right hand. It's a symbol of something, but what?

Verse 20 tells us that the 7 candlesticks represent the churches. The 7 stars are the angels, or messengers, of those churches. Some scholars believe these "messengers," the root meaning for the word we translate as "angels," is actually referring to pastors. If we consider the responsibility of that ministry position, we can easily see how they should be in the hand of Jesus.

The candlesticks are the churches, and we are to see Jesus walking in their midst. Jesus said, "Where two or three are gathered together in My name, I am there in the midst of them" (Matthew 18:20). If we are part of a true New Testament church, we can be confident as we are worshipping the Lord – if we are candlesticks, letting our light shine – that we are not alone.

Jesus is in the midst of the church, and the pastor is in His hand.

Section II

The Present

Chapter 2

In Chapter 2, we move to what was happening in the churches during John's lifetime.

The churches in the book of Revelation may be understood in several ways.

First, we have the *primary* interpretation, which identifies the churches as people gathering in specific first-century cities. That application is certainly valid.

Next, we have the *practical* application, which says these words are given to all churches for all time. This makes sense. From the first century until today, you can find churches around the world which have the characteristics of the churches described in the book of Revelation.

Finally, we have the *prophetic* revelation, which says the different churches represent segments of the church age.

From the very first century until now, these seven churches represent time periods when the majority of churches had the same characteristics. In the years AD 90–251, we can find the church of Ephesus being represented in the church culture. In the centuries that follow, we see further changes in the churches, represented by the conditions described for Smyrna, Pergamos, Thyatira, Sardis, Philadelphia, and Laodicea. If that interpretation is valid, we must now be living in the last church age.

Notice that the church in Thyatira lasted for a thousand years. Perhaps this last church age could be a thousand years as well. The Bible says "with the Lord one day is as a thousand years, and a thousand years as one day" (2 Peter 3:8). Our eternal God, with no beginning or end, has a perception of time that is different from ours.

The seven churches of Revelation are worthy of a separate, in-depth study, but here, a simple overview will be helpful. In the country we now call Turkey, other first-century churches existed, such as the churches in Colossae, Hierapolis, and Troas, which are mentioned in the Bible but not in the book of Revelation.

Let's read about the first church to be described.

[1] "To the angel of the church of Ephesus write,

'These things says He who holds the seven stars in His right hand, who walks in the midst of the seven golden lampstands: [2] "I know your works, your labor, your patience, and that you cannot bear those who are evil. And you have tested those who say they are apostles and are not, and have found them liars; [3] and you have persevered and have patience, and have labored for My name's sake and have not become weary. [4] Nevertheless I have this against you, that you have left your first love. [5] Remember therefore from where you have fallen; repent and do the first works, or else I will come to you quickly and remove your lampstand from its place – unless you repent. [6] But this you have, that you hate the deeds of the Nicolaitans, which I also hate.

[7] "He who has an ear, let him hear what the Spirit

says to the churches. To him who overcomes I will give to eat from the tree of life, which is in the midst of the Paradise of God.'"

In the first verse, Jesus salutes the Ephesian church, bringing greetings to the pastor. In verses 2, 3, and 6, the church members' work is commended – how people stood for truth and opposed evildoers, the Nicolaitans. Who were they? Some scholars believe they were people who followed the teachings of Nicolas, in a period identified as the "laity-ruled" church.

> *We should never feel like we're in a position to decide which parts of His Word we should follow*

Baptists believe in a democratic process in making church decisions called "congregational church government." I believe that's a good biblical way to manage church affairs, but we need to realize that God's church is a *theocracy*, not a *democracy*. We don't vote God in or out. We should never feel like we're in a position to decide which parts of His Word we should follow and which parts can be ignored.

Jesus is the head of His church. While He allows us to pray through and make decisions from our hearts and with our minds, He rules, which is what we mean by saying He is our "Lord." He's the Master Planner, calling all the shots and making the final call. Unfortunately, like the Ephesian church, we can easily slip into running church like a business, doing what makes sense to us instead of regarding Christ as our head.

The word *Nicolaitan* comes from two Greek words. One you will recognize right off – *nike*, the famous brand for athletic shoes and gear, which means "victory." The second word is *laos*, which means "lay people."

So the lay people were the ones who threatened Jesus' authority in the church at Ephesus, but the people said, "No we're not going to allow that to happen here. Jesus, you're the boss."

Even with that resolve, a condemnation comes in verse 4, because their love had faded. The honeymoon was over, and their primary focus had shifted to other concerns. No longer were they so strongly committed to their "first love." The Ephesian church had fallen "out of love" with Jesus.

In verse 5, Jesus exhorts the people to remember and repent or be prepared to see His presence removed from their church. Removing the lampstand from its place was a threat to take away their source of light, the presence of the Spirit of God.

Finally, in verse 7, we have the challenge: "He who has an ear, let him hear what the Spirit says," which is to listen with our hearts as well our ears. A spiritual hearing is important because the overcomers will "eat from the tree of life, which is in the midst of the Paradise of God." Those in the church who will remember, repent, and return to their first love will enjoy the presence of the Lord.

Beginning in verse 8, we find Smyrna, the *hurting* church.

8 "And to the angel of the church in Smyrna write,

'These things says the First and the Last, who was dead, and came to life: 9 "I know your works, tribulation, and poverty (but you are rich); and I know the blasphemy of those who say they are Jews and are not, but are a synagogue of Satan. 10 Do not fear any of those things which you are about to suffer. Indeed, the devil is about to throw some of you into prison, that you may be tested, and you will have tribulation ten days. Be faithful until death, and I will give you the crown of life.

11 "He who has an ear, let him hear what the Spirit

says to the churches. He who overcomes shall not be hurt by the second death.'"

This is the shortest letter to a church, but that doesn't diminish its significance. Unlike the other letters, this one has no condemnation, no words of reprimand.

The church in Smyrna was hurting and enduring severe persecution, which was characteristic of the churches during the last days of the Roman Empire. The Emperor Diocletian, officials of the Roman government, and unbelieving Jews were doing their best to stamp out Christianity in its infancy, as if it were a cancer that must be removed to preserve the health of its pagan society.

The word *Smyrna* comes from the word *myrrh* which means "bitter." Myrrh was a sweet-smelling gum resin derived from a small, thorny tree. You may remember that the wise men brought gifts to the baby Jesus – gold, frankincense and myrrh (Matthew 2).

To Smyrna, the myrrh church, Jesus identifies Himself as the Resurrected Lord, the Eternal One who was from the beginning and is forevermore, the First and the Last, the One who was dead and came to life. His identity is more than an Easter theme, because we see it throughout the Bible. Every day of our lives, we should recognize Him, our Resurrected Lord.

In verse 9, we see that the church has a reputation known by the Lord. He knows what every church is like. He knew what the church in Smyrna had been going through. He knows about us as well, both collectively and individually.

In the next verse, the church is told their persecution was for ten days, and their reward was coming. How long was the "ten days"? Perhaps it was a short period, or it could be the ten Great Persecutions that began with Nero and ended with Diocletian, a span of about two hundred years.

A crown of life was promised for those who refused to deny their faith in Christ, even unto death – a martyr's crown. So they aren't really dying, not spiritually, because they are rescued by the Lord. They are the overcomers who will not be hurt by the second death. This is the *hurting* church.

Beginning in verse 12, we read about the third church, the church at Pergamos, which is the *compromising* church. We might be living in the Pergamos church age. The word *pergamos* means "married." The church has been likened to "the bride of Christ," but this church had been unfaithful. To avoid persecution, they had compromised with the world.

¹² "And to the angel of the church in Pergamos write,

'These things says He who has the sharp two-edged sword: ¹³ "I know your works, and where you dwell, where Satan's throne is. And you hold fast to My name, and did not deny My faith even in the days in which Antipas was My faithful martyr, who was killed among you, where Satan dwells. ¹⁴ But I have a few things against you, because you have there those who hold the doctrine of Balaam, who taught Balak to put a stumbling block before the children of Israel, to eat things sacrificed to idols, and to commit sexual immorality. ¹⁵ Thus you also have those who hold the doctrine of the Nicolaitans, which thing I hate. ¹⁶ Repent, or else I will come to you quickly and will fight against them with the sword of My mouth.

¹⁷ "He who has an ear, let him hear what the Spirit says to the churches. To him who overcomes I will give some of the hidden manna to eat. And I will give him a white stone, and on the stone a new

name written which no one knows except him who receives it."'

Verse 12 speaks of the sword Jesus holds, sharp and double-edged, a symbol of judgment and authority. Next we learn about Satan's seat and how they stood firm against his assault, with Antipas suffering a martyr's death.

In verse 14, we're introduced to the stumbling block, referring to the story of Balaam in Numbers 22–25, who encouraged the Israelites to sin. As with the doctrine of Balaam, sin was something which could be tolerated in the Pergamos church. Not only had they slipped into false worship, but also they were following the practices of the Nicolaitans, giving the people the authority in the church – placing the people above the Lord Jesus, who should have been the head. The people were following what they wanted to do.

> Jesus will come quickly and fight against these people using the sword of His mouth.

I once pastored in a church where a decision needed to be made in a leadership meeting. "Well," I said, "this is what the Bible says we should do."

A man on the other side of the table said, "I don't care what the Bible says. We've been doing it all these years, and we'll keep doing it." I believe that's the spirit of the Nicolaitans – the will of man superseding the will of God.

Verse 16 reveals the swift judgment that will come. Jesus will come quickly and fight against these people using the sword of His mouth. In the next verse, He says, "If you have your antenna up, and if you are connected to your spiritual Wi-Fi link, then pay attention to what the Spirit is saying. He'll give you 'angel food'."

The white stone in verse 17 had specific meaning in the first century. Whenever an accused person appeared at trial for a crime, the judge would show evidence of his verdict with either a black stone or a white stone. A black stone indicated guilt, but a white stone emphasized the person's innocence. Jesus was telling those who would listen that they should repent and be the overcomers. He said, "I will give you a white stone with your name written on it so everyone will know you have been found innocent."

Verses 18–29 describe the church in Thyatira, the *corrupt* church.

[18] "And to the angel of the church in Thyatira write,

'These things says the Son of God, who has eyes like a flame of fire, and His feet like fine brass: [19] "I know your works, love, service, faith, and your patience; and as for your works, the last are more than the first. [20] Nevertheless I have a few things against you, because you allow that woman Jezebel, who calls herself a prophetess, to teach and seduce My servants to commit sexual immorality and eat things sacrificed to idols. [21] And I gave her time to repent of her sexual immorality, and she did not repent. [22] Indeed I will cast her into a sickbed, and those who commit adultery with her into great tribulation, unless they repent of their deeds. [23] I will kill her children with death, and all the churches shall know that I am He who searches the minds and hearts. And I will give to each one of you according to your works.

[24] "Now to you I say, and to the rest in Thyatira, as many as do not have this doctrine, who have not known the depths of Satan, as they say, I will put on you no other burden. [25] But hold fast what you have

till I come. ²⁶ And he who overcomes, and keeps My works until the end, to him I will give power over the nations –

²⁷ 'He shall rule them with a rod of iron;

They shall be dashed to pieces like the potter's vessels' – as I also have received from My Father; ²⁸ and I will give him the morning star.

²⁹ "He who has an ear, let him hear what the Spirit says to the churches."'

You may remember a woman named Lydia in Acts Chapter 16, who came from Thyatira. Originally from Greece, she is thought to be the first Christian convert from Europe, a merchant of high-priced clothing, a "seller of purple," as the Bible puts it. Thyatira was known for its clothing industry. Its commerce was fueled by pagan worship. Evidently, the church had succumbed to the lure of the culture. We see some of that in the United States today.

Verse 18 reveals the powerful Christ, and the next verses express some of the positive attributes of the church in Thyatira, followed by its pluralistic beliefs. They were saying, "Anything goes. It really doesn't matter how you live or what you do or what you believe."

Beginning in verse 24, we see the promises of the coming age – what Jesus said was going to happen. One day He would be given power over the nations. He would rule with a rod of iron. The people needed to follow Him so they would be winners in the end.

From time to time, our own future looks bleak. But because we've read this last book of the Bible, we should know we're going to win in the end.

Chapter 3

In the first six verses of Chapter 3, we see the church at Sardis, which was the *dead* church.

I don't want to offend anyone, but it is a wonder to me why people would name their church Sardis Baptist Church. Even if I lived in Sardis, Mississippi, I think I would choose a different name. We want to identify ourselves with the living, not the dead.

> [1] "And to the angel of the church in Sardis write,
>
> 'These things says He who has the seven Spirits of God and the seven stars: "I know your works, that you have a name that you are alive, but you are dead. [2] Be watchful, and strengthen the things which remain, that are ready to die, for I have not found your works perfect before God [3] Remember therefore how you have received and heard; hold fast and repent. Therefore if you will not watch, I will come upon you as a thief, and you will not know what hour I will come upon you. [4] You have a few names even in Sardis who have not defiled their garments; and they shall walk with Me in white, for they are

worthy. ⁵ He who overcomes shall be clothed in white garments, and I will not blot out his name from the Book of Life; but I will confess his name before My Father and before His angels.

⁶ "He who has an ear, let him hear what the Spirit says to the churches.'"

The church at Sardis has a name for being alive when it's actually dead. It sees itself as rich and righteous, prosperous and in good health. There's the reputation and then there's the reality. The reputation is that the church is doing great. But in reality, the church is dead.

The remedy comes in the second verse. Jesus is calling the people to repentance, because they have drifted *away* from God. They have not moved *toward* God.

Drifting always moves people away from God, because that action takes the line of least resistance. If we desire Him and want to seek Him, we face an uphill climb – a daily struggle.

From Sunday to Sunday, your church will not get more spiritual by drifting through the motions of what it has done before. Churches become spiritually alive only when there is a commitment to get into the Word, stay with the Word, and live the Word. Through His Word, we let the living Lord Jesus live through us.

Sardis had somehow forgotten the remedy. But not everyone had forgotten. Notice in verses 4–6 that there is always a remnant. These are people who individually maintain a living relationship with the Lord among a gathering which lacks spiritual life.

The light of churches can go out. The building is open, and people come to be a part of the program. They have a form of godliness, but they lack the spiritual light. As the apostle Paul warned: they have a form of godliness but deny its power (2 Timothy 3:5).

If Jesus removes the candlestick, the presence of the Spirit, that church dies, even though its members still attend and participate in activities. There may be singing and preaching and praying. But if He has removed His Spirit from that church, it is nothing more than a *a dead church has no approval rating with Jesus.* country club with a steeple on top. It's not a real spiritual entity.

A sad closing note on this church is the lack of any commendation. Sardis received no praise, because a dead church has no approval rating with Jesus.

We need more churches like the one at Philadelphia, which we read about next.

[7] "And to the angel of the church in Philadelphia write,

'These things says He who is holy, He who is true, "He who has the key of David, He who opens and no one shuts, and shuts and no one opens": [8] "I know your works. See, I have set before you an open door, and no one can shut it; for you have a little strength, have kept My word, and have not denied My name. [9] Indeed I will make those of the synagogue of Satan, who say they are Jews and are not, but lie – indeed I will make them come and worship before your feet, and to know that I have loved you. [10] Because you have kept My command to persevere, I also will keep you from the hour of trial which shall come upon the whole world, to test those who dwell on the earth. [11] Behold, I am coming quickly! Hold fast what you have, that no one may take your crown. [12] He who overcomes, I will make him a pillar in the temple of My God, and he shall go out no more. And I will write on him the name of My God and the name of the city of My God, the New Jerusalem, which comes down out of heaven from My God. And I will write on him My new name.

¹³ "He who has an ear, let him hear what the Spirit says to the churches.'"

This is the church of the *open door*. The word *Philadelphia* comes from two Greek words. *Phileo* means "love," and *delphia* refers to "brothers." Together, we should translate the meaning literally as "brotherly love." This church characterizes the cooperative attitudes that prevail in true Spirit-filled churches. People were working together, helping one another, caring for one another.

In verse 7, we see that the presence of the Lord is in this place. In the verses following, we should not be surprised to read about the Lord's plans for this church and the promise to those who were faithful. This was a church on the move. This was a church with an open door. This was a church making a difference in the community. They were doing what they could do, and God was using them. This church experienced the blessings of the Lord like none of the others.

Some have said this church represents the great time of missionary outreach beginning in the 1700s and ending in the 1900s, when Christian communities showed a relentless passion to fulfill the Great Commission and spread the Gospel around the world. The church was especially blessed by the strong assemblies in Europe and in North America, which spread to other countries as well.

Beginning in verse 14, we see the last of the seven churches, the church of Laodicea.

¹⁴ "And to the angel of the church of the Laodiceans write,

'These things says the Amen, the Faithful and True Witness, the Beginning of the creation of God: ¹⁵ "I know your works, that you are neither cold nor hot. I could wish you were cold or hot. ¹⁶ So then, because you are lukewarm, and neither cold nor hot, I will vomit you out of My mouth. ¹⁷ Because you say, 'I am rich, have become wealthy, and have need of nothing' – and do not know that you are wretched, miserable, poor, blind, and naked – ¹⁸ I counsel you to buy from Me gold refined in the fire, that you may be rich; and white garments, that you may be clothed, that the shame of your nakedness may not be revealed; and anoint your eyes with eye salve, that you may see. ¹⁹ As many as I love, I rebuke and chasten. Therefore be zealous and repent. ²⁰ Behold, I stand at the door and knock. If anyone hears My voice and opens the door, I will come in to him and dine with him, and he with Me. ²¹ To him who overcomes I will grant to sit with Me on My throne, as I also overcame and sat down with My Father on His throne.

²² "He who has an ear, let him hear what the Spirit says to the churches.""""

This is the *disgusting* church. The name *Laodicea* means the "rule of the people." A pastor should not usurp the Lord's position and make himself the great shepherd over God's flock. Neither should the people place their own desires above the will of the Lord Jesus. But this is exactly what happened, because the Laodiceans forgot that the church is to be a theocracy where Jesus is the Head.

Verse 14 declares that Jesus is in charge of His church. He is the Amen, the Faithful, the Witness, the Beginning of creation. He is our all in all. The problems are introduced in verses 15–17: apathy and arrogance. In the two verses after that, you have the proposal.

> *Without him, we can stuff our stomachs full and still not be satisfied.*

Laodicea was a major banking center in the region with vast gold reserves. Out of the fertile Lycus valley came black glossy wool that produced expensive carpets and luxurious clothing. A medical school in Laodicea specialized in the treatment of eye diseases. Jesus looks at each of those areas and speaks of their true value, pointing out that they were not as well off as they thought they were. "You're lacking in all these," Jesus said. By saying they had no needs, they became blind to their need for Christ.

The United States has been blessed with riches more than anywhere else in the world. We have bigger buildings, more technology, and more money. Of all people, the American church is in a position to look at its wealth and the abundance of its possessions and say, "I have need of nothing." But rich as we are with worldly goods, we can be living in poverty, lacking what we need most – that which truly satisfies.

Jesus said we would not find life in the abundance of our possessions (Luke 12:15), and He was right. He is the Bread of Life (John 6:35). Without him, we can stuff our stomachs full and still not be satisfied. We can have everything we could possibly want, everything we can imagine, but without Christ at work in our lives, we have nothing.

We need the power of the Holy Spirit of God exploding outward from where we are – in our neighborhoods, our cities, our states, and our nation. I fear we may be the Laodicean church, the disgusting church, where Jesus said, "You're neither hot nor cold. You make me sick to my stomach, and I'm going to throw up." That's the Richards translation of how Jesus expressed His displeasure when He said if we were lukewarm as a church, He would spew us out of His mouth.

We often use verse 20 to invite people to receive Jesus into their lives.

Jesus is standing at our heart's door, knocking. If any man hears His voice and opens the door, He will come in. That is a biblical truism about receiving Christ for salvation. But here, it's talking about the church. Jesus is on the outside of the church, knocking on the door, asking to come in. He promises fellowship and favor to those who will let Him in the church.

At the close of the church age, the church digresses to a point of apathy, uselessness, and inactivity. There will be a faithful few who will be here when Jesus comes.

Next, we will take a look into Heaven, because the next chapter speaks of our future. Jesus is coming to take to Himself those who are the redeemed.

Section III

The Future

Chapter 4

In this chapter, we are taking a trip to Heaven. People have different views about the return of Jesus, but verse 1 describes the time when the redeemed are caught away to be with the Lord.

> [1] After these things, I looked, and behold, a door standing open in heaven. And the first voice which I heard was like a trumpet speaking with me, saying, "Come up here, and I will show you things which must take place after this."

> [2] Immediately I was in the Spirit; and behold, a throne set in heaven, and One sat on the throne. [3] And He who sat there was like a jasper and a sardius stone in appearance; and there was a rainbow around the throne, in appearance like an emerald. [4] Around the throne were twenty-four thrones, and on the thrones I saw twenty-four elders sitting, clothed in white robes; and they had crowns of gold on their heads. [5] And from the throne proceeded lightnings, thunderings, and voices. Seven lamps of fire were burning before the throne, which are the seven Spirits of God.

⁶ Before the throne there was a sea of glass, like crystal. And in the midst of the throne, and around the throne, were four living creatures full of eyes in front and in back. ⁷ The first living creature was like a lion, the second living creature like a calf, the third living creature had a face like a man, and the fourth living creature was like a flying eagle. ⁸ The four living creatures, each having six wings, were full of eyes around and within. And they do not rest day or night, saying:

> "Holy, holy, holy,
> Lord God Almighty,
> Who was and is and is to come!"

⁹ Whenever the living creatures give glory and honor and thanks to Him who sits on the throne, who lives forever and ever, ¹⁰ the twenty-four elders fall down before Him who sits on the throne and worship Him who lives forever and ever, and cast their crowns before the throne, saying:

> ¹¹ "You are worthy, O Lord,
> To receive glory and honor and power;
> For You created all things,
> And by Your will they exist and were created."

There are two phases to the second coming of Jesus. First, He comes *for* His saints, and then He comes *with* His saints. He comes *for* His saints in what we call "the rapture," the catching away of the redeemed, which could happen at any moment, even today. On earth, seven years of tribulation will follow. At the end of the tribulation period, Jesus will come with His saints, those of us who are redeemed, back to this earth to right all the wrongs and to rule and reign as king.

At His time and good pleasure, God will bring an end to this age. While we do not know exactly when that time will be, God has given us some information about our future. One day all Christians will be carried into Heaven. The next event on God's agenda is the return of Jesus. There are no Scriptures which have yet to be fulfilled. The temple in Jerusalem doesn't have to be built. We don't have to look for signs. All we have to do is listen for the sound.

> *While we do not know exactly when that time will be, God has given us some information about our future.*

In verse 1, we hear the sound of the trumpet. John is caught up to Heaven to get the rest of his revelation, and he symbolizes the redeemed when he is caught up. In the nine verses that follow, we get a view of the throne, mentioned twelve times in this chapter. This is where Jesus is seated, on the Father's throne, surrounded by majesty. There are ministers around the throne.

Those living creatures John describes here are also found in Ezekiel 1 and Numbers 2.

Then we have the Master, seated on the throne.

Finally, we are given a statement about the One who is on the throne. I like how the King James Version translates this last verse. "Thou hast created all things, and for thy pleasure they are and were created." He is our Creator. We exist for His pleasure.

In this chapter, we are worshipping Jesus as the Creator of all.

Chapter 5

In Chapter 5, we are worshipping Jesus as the Redeemer of all.

¹ And I saw in the right hand of Him who sat on the throne a scroll written inside and on the back, sealed with seven seals. ² Then I saw a strong angel proclaiming with a loud voice, "Who is worthy to open the scroll and to loose its seals?" ³ And no one in heaven or on the earth or under the earth was able to open the scroll, or to look at it.

⁴ So I wept much, because no one was found worthy to open and read the scroll, or to look at it. ⁵ But one of the elders said to me, "Do not weep. Behold, the Lion of the tribe of Judah, the Root of David, has prevailed to open the scroll and to loose its seven seals."

⁶ And I looked, and behold, in the midst of the throne and of the four living creatures, and in the midst of the elders, stood a Lamb as though it had been slain, having seven horns and seven eyes, which are the seven Spirits of God sent out into all the earth. ⁷ Then He came and took the scroll out of the right hand of Him who sat on the throne.

⁸ Now when He had taken the scroll, the four living creatures and the twenty-four elders fell down before the Lamb, each having a harp, and golden bowls full of incense, which are the prayers of the saints. ⁹ And they sang a new song, saying:

> "You are worthy to take the scroll
> And to open its seals;
> For You were slain,
> And have redeemed us to God by Your blood
> Out of every tribe and tongue and people
> and nation,
> ¹⁰ And have made us kings and priests to our God;
> And we shall reign on the earth."

¹¹ Then I looked, and I heard the voice of many angels around the throne, the living creatures, and the elders; and the number of them was ten thousand times ten thousand, and thousands of thousands, ¹² saying with a loud voice:

> "Worthy is the Lamb who was slain
> To receive power and riches and wisdom,
> And strength and honor and glory and blessing!"

¹³ And every creature which is in heaven and on the earth and under the earth and such as are in the sea, and all that are in them, I heard saying:

> "Blessing and honor and glory and power
> Be to Him who sits on the throne,
> And to the Lamb, forever and ever!"

¹⁴ Then the four living creatures said, "Amen!" And

the twenty-four elders fell down and worshipped
Him who lives forever and ever.

Here we have Heaven, a place beyond our comprehension,
and we will be there with Jesus. John saw Jesus worthy of all
recognition for His redemptive church, and the people will
worship Him.

In the first four verses, we have *the unopened book*. The right
to rule in Heaven and reveal the end-time events is found in the
ability to open this book. There were
many who might have tried to open
the book, but they had no right to
touch the cover. Only one was found
worthy to open the book: Jesus.

He is the perfect king.
Look for Jesus.

In verses 5–7, we find the unnoticed Lamb. Jesus was there
all along, overlooked by John. But Jesus the Lamb is the one
made king. He is the perfect king. Look for Jesus.

We see unrestrained worship in verses 8–14. Supplication,
song, and shouting will all be a part of worship in Heaven. A
great day is coming when we will see Him face to face. Each
day on earth, we can celebrate the resurrection of Christ, but in
Heaven we will recognize Him directly with our praise because
we, like John, will see our risen Lord.

Before we move to the next chapter, we should quickly review
what we have seen thus far.

Chapter 1 introduced the book, displaying a beautiful snapshot of the Lord Jesus, who is giving the revelation to John, the
scribe who will write the revelation of Jesus Christ on these
pages for everyone to read and understand. Verse 19 handed
us the key to the book, an index to the three sections: (1) The
Past, containing what John had already seen, (2) The Present,
in Chapters 2 and 3, interpreting what was happening then,
and (3) The Future, in the remainder of the book, revealing
what lies ahead.

Chapters 2 and 3 showed us the seven churches of Asia, which could be typical of churches at any time during the church age. Or they could represent different periods of the church age. We could be living in the Laodicean church age, the last period before Jesus comes.

Chapters 4 and 5 open our eyes to the future. The trumpet sounds. When a voice from Heaven says, "Come up here," John rises in his vision into the presence of the Lord to receive the revelation. His rising is a pre-figure of the rapture of all the believers when Jesus comes in the clouds, which ends the church age and begins the tribulation.

We see what worship will be like in Heaven. In Chapter 4, God is worshipped as our creator. Jesus is exalted as Creator and Owner of all things. Then in Chapter 5, Jesus is worshipped as our Redeemer who cleansed our sins, restored our relationship with the Father, and made it possible for us to join Christ in Heaven. As we read these verses, we can imagine ourselves becoming part of these wonderful, beautiful scenes of worship in the presence of the Lord. We can taste the joy of the coming of the Lord and sense Heaven's glory.

Remember, the second coming of Jesus Christ has two phases: The first phase begins when Jesus comes *for* His saints, which could happen any moment. It could happen today, and we need to think about how wonderful that day will be. Imagine your voice among the millions surrounding His throne, joining every creature in sharing God's glory, singing, "Blessing and honor and glory and power." Whether it happens now or later, we know that day in Heaven will come.

Seven years later, Jesus will return to earth with His saints. This is the second phase of His second coming, when Jesus literally comes back to this earth and makes all things right. Jesus then will be the Lord over this earth. He will be king. He will rule and reign for a thousand years.

Chapter 6

The seven years of tribulation are introduced in Chapter 6. This is the time between the rapture of the redeemed and the reign of Christ on the earth, when God's wrath is poured out on this world and He deals with the Jewish people.

The time leading up to the tribulation is known as the "Fullness of the Gentiles." Until the rapture, the Gentile world leads the religious and spiritual aspects of God's kingdom. But after the rapture, the Jews will once again step into the forefront as the world's religious leaders. The focus will be upon them as the ones God is primarily dealing with. Again, this is known as the "Fullness of the Gentiles," as referenced in Matthew 21:45 and in Romans 11:25.

In the first two verses, we see someone who looks like Christ.

> ¹ Now I saw when the Lamb opened one of the seals; and I heard one of the four living creatures saying with a voice like thunder, "Come and see." ² And I looked, and behold, a white horse. He who sat on it had a bow; and a crown was given to him, and he went out conquering and to conquer.

Remember, Jesus is the one opening the seals, the worthy one who has the right and authority to open the book. Therefore, we should not be surprised to learn that the one riding the white horse is someone other than Jesus.

Because the rider sits on a white horse and wears a crown, going out to conquer, people are sometimes led to think this must be Jesus. But no, we see Jesus much later in Chapter 19, coming on a white horse, with a crown. Here, we have the first identification of the false christ, the Antichrist, who is called "the beast" in Chapter 13.

there will be those who cry, "Peace, peace," and then sudden destruction will come upon them.

While Jesus is opening the seals, the imitation of Christ wears a crown, indicating his ruling over the people by their consent. When he comes onto the scene, conquering and to conquer, he will exhibit the type of personality people will simply give in to, following blindly, willing to have him rule their lives.

In the next two verses, as Jesus opens the second of seven seals, we see the beginning of a fatal conflict.

> [3] When He opened the second seal, I heard the second living creature saying, "Come and see." [4] Another horse, fiery red, went out. And it was granted to the one who sat on it to take peace from the earth, and that people should kill one another; and there was given to him a great sword.

Red is the symbol of blood. The sword symbolizes war. This false peace ushered in by the Antichrist is destined for collapse in the middle of the tribulation. For three-and-a-half years, the kingdom of the Antichrist appears to enjoy some type of peace. This condition is foretold in 1 Thessalonians 5:3, which says there will be those who cry, "Peace, peace," and then sudden destruction will come upon them.

The false christ has come forth. He has brought a kind of peace that is not real and cannot last. Then the fatal conflict begins, the war to end all wars.

In the next two verses, we see an economic crash, the failure of the world economy.

> [5] When He opened the third seal, I heard the third living creature say, "Come and see." So I looked, and behold, a black horse, and he who sat on it had a pair of scales in his hand. [6] And I heard a voice in the midst of the four living creatures saying, "A quart of wheat for a denarius, and three quarts of barley for a denarius; and do not harm the oil and the wine."

Some have projected the cost of a loaf of bread will equal a day's wages. To get an idea what that day would be like, take your household income for a week and divide that number by seven. That amount would be enough to buy only one loaf of bread, not enough to feed the family, let alone pay for other necessities.

The oil and wine are not to be touched. What does that mean? One interpretation is that the cost of bare essentials, represented by the bread, will leave no money for buying any luxuries, so the oil and wine will be in abundance because nobody can afford to buy any. Or it might be that the wealthy will not suffer as much as the common people. I think we can identify with either interpretation and see how they could be true.

As the fourth seal is opened in verse 7, we see fearful calamities coming.

> [7] When He opened the fourth seal, I heard the voice of the fourth living creature saying, "Come and see." [8] So I looked, and behold, a pale horse. And the

REVELATION: THE BEST IS YET TO COME

name of him who sat on it was Death, and Hades followed with him. And power was given to them over
a fourth of the earth, to kill with sword, with hunger,
with death, and by the beasts of the earth.

The beasts could be the kings of the earth or it could actually
mean the animals. Whatever it is, we know death will come
from various sources. This is the
we know death will come passage you may have heard about
from various sources. when there is a reference to the "four
horsemen of the apocalypse." Here
are the calamities, the fearful calamities, which come upon
people during this terrible time of tribulation.

In verse 9, we learn about the faithful Christians.

> [9] When he opened the fifth seal, I saw under the altar
> the souls of those who had been slain for the word of
> God and for the testimony which they held. [10] And
> they cried with a loud voice, saying, "How long, O
> Lord, holy and true, until You judge and avenge our
> blood on those who dwell on the earth?" [11] Then a
> white robe was given to each of them; and it was said
> to them that they should rest a little while longer,
> until both the number of their fellow servants and
> their brethren, who would be killed as they were, was
> completed.

Here we find the tribulation martyrs – the people on earth
who gave their lives to Christ, who trusted Jesus during this
time of tribulation after the rapture. Yes, some people will be
saved during the tribulation period.

Earlier, the church-age martyrs were told to "turn the other
cheek." Jesus said, "Love your enemies, bless those who curse

you, do good to those who hate you, and pray for those who spitefully use you and persecute you" (Matthew 5:44). While the deacon Stephen was being stoned, as he breathed his last, he prayed, "Lord, do not charge them with this sin" (Acts 7:60). During the church age, we're told *not* to retaliate against evil done to us.

But during the tribulation period, the saints are praying for retribution, crying out for vengeance, for justice. They're praying for the power of God, in His wrath and anger, to be poured out on these who have brought death and destruction.

The tribulation saints await their resurrection. There are three parts to the first resurrection mentioned in Revelation 20:6. These resurrections correspond to the harvests mentioned in the Old Testament. Christ is the first fruits as mentioned in 1 Corinthians 15:20. Those who are resurrected at His coming are the general harvest. The resurrection of the tribulation saints will be the *gleanings*.

Beginning in verse 12, we see the final condemnation.

> ¹² I looked when He opened the sixth seal, and behold, there was a great earthquake; and the sun became black as sackcloth of hair, and the moon became like blood. ¹³ And the stars of heaven fell to the earth, as a fig tree drops its late figs when it is shaken by a mighty wind. ¹⁴ Then the sky receded as a scroll when it is rolled up, and every mountain and island was moved out of its place. ¹⁵ And the kings of the earth, the great men, the rich men, the commanders, the mighty men, every slave and every free man, hid themselves in the caves and in the rocks of the mountains, ¹⁶ and said to the mountains and rocks, "Fall on us and hide us from the face of Him who sits on the throne and from the wrath of the

Lamb! [17] For the great day of His wrath has come,
and who is able to stand?"

In this final condemnation, our planet Earth will experience
physical convulsions. Today we see meteors streak across the
sky in a flash of brilliant light. We watch the asteroids, fearful
one might enter Earth's atmosphere and wreak more devasta-
tion than a hundred atomic bombs. Verse 13 tells us the stars
of heaven will fall to the earth.

Prophets of old said this would happen. Passages in Joel
Chapter 2 and Isaiah Chapter 13 tell about the final condemnation which will come to those who stand against the Lord.
Jesus said, "Immediately after the tribulation of those days the
sun will be darkened, and the moon will not give its light; the
stars will fall from heaven, and the powers of the heavens will
be shaken" (Matthew 24:29).

In Exodus Chapter 10, we read about a time when the sun
was darkened during God's judgment. The Egyptians could not
see their hands in front of their faces. The noontime sky was as
midnight with no light from the moon or stars.

When Jesus hung on the cross and our sins were placed
upon Him, He became the ultimate sin bearer, One who knew
no sin (Matthew 27:45). At that time, the sun was darkened in
the middle of the day.

Here in the tribulation, the final condemnation of this earth
will take place. There will be cataclysmic events and topographi-
cal changes brought upon the earth. The trauma upon the earth
is so great at the conclusion of the sixth seal that people are
begging to die but they cannot. They pray for rocks to fall upon
them, yet they persist in refusing to let Jesus be their Lord and
Savior. This shows how hardened the human heart can be. Just
as Pharaoh's heart was hardened, so it will be in these people
during the tribulation. Perhaps they could be saved, but they
choose not to be. They would rather die than be saved.

Chapter 7

C hapter 7 is a parenthetic chapter which precedes the open-ing of the last seal in Chapter 8. Here, we see more of the terrible times during the tribulation and how God deals with the Jews.

The Jews were to be sealed so they could serve Him in a special way.

Scholars have different opinions about who the 144,000 are. I believe they are the evangelists for the Gospel during the tribulation period. This is a Heaven scene. There will also be Gentiles saved during the tribulation period.

There is a suspension of the plagues coming on the earth during the tribulation time to give an opportunity for God's servants and God's people to be marked.

> [1] After these things I saw four angels standing at the four corners of the earth, holding the four winds of the earth, that the wind should not blow on the earth, on the sea, or on any tree. [2] Then I saw another angel ascending from the east, having the seal of the living God. And he cried with a loud voice to the four angels to whom it was granted to harm the earth and the sea, [3] saying, "Do not harm the earth, the sea, or the trees till we have sealed the servants of our God on their foreheads."

This seal was a permanent identification showing that a transaction had been completed. During the tribulation period, just as the Antichrist will mark his followers with "the mark of the beast," the followers of Jesus will be marked.

We see the preferred people numbered in verses 4–8.

> 4 And I heard the number of those who were sealed. One hundred and forty-four thousand of all the tribes of the children of Israel were sealed:
> 5 of the tribe of Judah twelve thousand were sealed, of the tribe of Reuben twelve thousand were sealed; of the tribe of Gad twelve thousand were sealed;
> 6 of the tribe of Asher twelve thousand were sealed; of the tribe of Naphtali twelve thousand were sealed; of the tribe of Manasseh twelve thousand were sealed;
> 7 of the tribe of Simeon twelve thousand were sealed; of the tribe of Levi twelve thousand were sealed; of the tribe of Issachar twelve thousand were sealed;
> 8 of the tribe of Zebulun twelve thousand were sealed; of the tribe of Joseph twelve thousand were sealed; of the tribe of Benjamin twelve thousand were sealed.

Over the centuries, the tribes of Israel have been lost. But medical science has made amazing strides in DNA research. We can now trace our own ancestry by just a little swab in the mouth. I believe it will be possible to identify the tribes one day through some type of process. Even without it, God knows who they are. God is able to designate them in their proper tribes.

The Bible tells us the tribes will be restored back to the land. In Isaiah 49:5–6, we have the promise that the land will be divided by the tribes. Jesus said the tribes would be distinct in the new age. Explaining to His disciples what would happen, He said, "Assuredly I say to you, that in the regeneration, when the Son of Man sits on the throne of His glory, you who have followed Me will also sit on twelve thrones, judging the twelve tribes of Israel" (Matthew 19:28).

If you compare the tribes of Chapter 7:5–8 with the listings in Numbers Chapter 2 and Ezekiel Chapter 48, you will find some differences. The book of Numbers lists the twelve tribes that entered the land of Israel. Ezekiel lists the tribes as they actually occupied the land. Here in Revelation, the 144,000 are listed as twelve tribes of 12,000 – the evangelists who will preach the Gospel and tell people, "Our Messiah has come, and He's coming back."

Dan and Ephraim are not listed in this group, making the tribe distinction different from other references. Possibly, those tribes are not listed because of their involvement in idolatry, so they are not used as evangelists during the tribulation period. Both Deuteronomy Chapter 29 and 1 Kings Chapter 12 express this concern.

Usually, Levi is not listed as a tribe, because they received their inheritance separately from across the land as priests. The tribe of Joseph is typically listed as two tribes with his sons' names, Ephraim and Manasseh. But here, Joseph is listed instead of Ephraim. We don't know the reason for the differences. What we do know is this is a preferred people God has chosen to use during this particular time.

Beginning in verse 9, we see praise for protection.

> [9] After these things I looked, and behold, a great multitude which no one could number, of all nations, tribes, peoples, and tongues, standing before the throne and before the Lamb, clothed with white robes, with palm branches in their hands, [10] and crying out with a loud voice, saying, "Salvation belongs to our God who sits on the throne and to the Lamb!"

¹¹ All the angels stood around the throne and the elders and the four living creatures, and fell on their faces before the throne and worshiped God, ¹² saying:

> "Amen! Blessing and glory and wisdom,
> Thanksgiving and honor and power and might,
> Be to our God forever and ever.
> Amen."

¹³ Then one of the elders answered, saying to me, "Who are these arrayed in white robes, and where did they come from?"

¹⁴ And I said to him, "Sir, you know."

So he said to me, "These are the ones who come out of the great tribulation, and washed their robes and made them white in the blood of the Lamb. ¹⁵ Therefore they are before the throne of God, and serve Him day and night in His temple. And He who sits on the throne will dwell among them. ¹⁶ They shall neither hunger anymore nor thirst anymore; the sun shall not strike them, nor any heat; ¹⁷ for the Lamb who is in the midst of the throne will shepherd them and lead them to living fountains of waters. And God will wipe away every tear from their eyes."

This is a time of praise and thanksgiving around the throne of God. A great multitude of Gentiles will be saved. Verse 9 says their number was too large to count, a great multitude of all the nations, tribes, people, and languages. This great multitude of Gentiles who are saved during the tribulation will worship around the throne of God.

Chapter 8

At this point we move back to the judgments, and they keep on coming.

> ¹ When he opened the seventh seal, there was silence in heaven for about half an hour.

Some people have made a joke, saying there will be no preachers in Heaven, because preachers like to talk so much. I'm not sure that's why there is silence in Heaven for half an hour.

It's a mystery. Perhaps everyone is just awestruck by the reality of the presence of a holy God. Maybe it's because of the viewing of the opening of the seals. There will be silence.

Next, we have the interceding in Heaven.

> ² And I saw the seven angels who stand before God, and to them were given seven trumpets. ³ Then another angel, having a golden censer, came and stood at the altar. He was given much incense, that he should offer it with the prayers of all the saints upon the golden altar which was before the throne. ⁴ And the smoke of the incense, with the prayers of the saints, ascended before God from the angel's hand. ⁵

Then the angel took the censer, filled it with fire from the altar, and threw it to the earth. And there were noises, thunderings, lightnings, and an earthquake.

In verse 2, seven angels are poised to sound their trumpets, which were used to announce war, worship, and judgment. The next verse talks about the prayers of the saints. These were obviously the prayers of the tribulation saints, which would be the vengeance prayer. As they were praying, God hears them and answers them, pouring out His wrath upon those who had persecuted these saints.

Beginning with verse 6, we see the indignation from Heaven. Remember, we have a total of seven seals. The seventh seal is the 7 trumpets.

6 So the seven angels who had the seven trumpets prepared themselves to sound.

7 The first angel sounded: And hail and fire followed, mingled with blood, and they were thrown to the earth. And a third of the trees were burned up, and all green grass was burned up.

8 Then the second angel sounded: And something like a great mountain burning with fire was thrown into the sea, and a third of the sea became blood. 9 And a third of the living creatures in the sea died, and a third of the ships were destroyed.

10 Then the third angel sounded: And a great star fell from heaven, burning like a torch, and it fell on a third of the rivers and on the springs of water. 11 The name of the star is Wormwood. A third of the waters

became wormwood, and many men died from the water, because it was made bitter.

¹² Then the fourth angel sounded: And a third of the sun was struck, a third of the moon, and a third of the stars, so that a third of them were darkened. A third of the day did not shine, and likewise the night.

¹³ And I looked, and I heard an angel flying through the midst of heaven, saying with a loud voice, "Woe, woe, woe to the inhabitants of the earth, because of the remaining blasts of the trumpet of the three angels who are about to sound!"

Four angels sounded their trumpets. In verses 6 and 7, we see the first trumpet of judgment: hail, fire, and blood. The trumpet judgments begin here in Chapter 8, and they don't end until Chapter 11. The words of the prophet Joel are being fulfilled. "And I will show wonders in the heavens and in the earth: Blood and fire and pillars of smoke. The sun shall be turned into darkness, and the moon into blood, before the coming of the great and awesome day of the Lord" (Joel 2:30–31).

There is no reason to interpret these verses as anything but literal.

During the tribulation, five of the ten Egyptian plagues are duplicated. This judgment is like the seventh plague found in Exodus Chapter 9, with hail, fire, and blood.

There is no reason to interpret these verses as anything but literal. Jesus walked on the water, the apostles raised the dead, and Jonah was swallowed by a fish. The supernatural phenomena that took place in the Old Testament and in apostolic times will once again be displayed on this earth.

In verses 8 and 9, we see the second trumpet, which is

REVELATION: THE BEST IS YET TO COME

"something like" a burning mountain, not to be taken literally as a mountain on fire. This is a metaphor John used to identify what he saw. This judgment corresponds with Exodus Chapter 7:19–21. The sea referred to here could very well be the Mediterranean Sea. We don't believe it would be all the seven seas of the world, but it could be localized in only the Mediterranean. Or it could be some other sea, but it does speak of the sea.

The judgment of wormwood is sounded with the third trumpet, in verses 10 and 11. The Old Testament speaks of how wormwood would be a judgment brought upon the people as the water would be bitter (Jeremiah 9:13–15).

We see the fourth trumpet sound in verse 12 – the sun, the moon, and the stars – which is a recurrence of the sixth seal back in Chapter 6. Some of the judgments are repeated. Some of them are simultaneous.

Finally in verse 13, an angelic judgment is spoken upon the earth, simply a continued acknowledgement that God is pouring out His wrath.

We truly live in an age of grace. I am so glad that God is merciful, gracious, forbearing, and patient. Otherwise, I would have been zapped like a mosquito hitting a bug-zapper light a long time ago. But God loves us, and He is longsuffering toward us.

The time will come when God says, "Enough is enough." Then He will bring His righteous judgment.

Chapter 9

Chapter 9 has three trumpets and three woes. The horror becomes more personal. John saw the torment of the people and the hardness of the human heart. In Chapter 9, the final three trumpets are sounded. These are the three woes spoken of in the last verse of the previous chapter.

Now we see the unlocking of the bottomless pit.

> [1] Then the fifth angel sounded: And I saw a star fallen from heaven to the earth. To him was given the key to the bottomless pit. [2] And he opened the bottomless pit, and smoke arose out of the pit like the smoke of a great furnace. So the sun and the air were darkened because of the smoke of the pit.

The star is a symbol used for an angel. We know that already from what we learned back in Chapter 1. He had to be an angel of God, because he had the key to the pit. The bottomless pit here is not Hell. Sometimes we read these phrases and terms, and we think of them synonymously. We may think of Hell, the Lake of Fire, and the bottomless pit as all being the same thing. But here, the bottomless pit is a prison house for demons. When Jesus encountered the maniac of Gadara, the demons possessing him said, "Don't send us to the pit" (Luke 8:31). They didn't want to go to that prison for demons, so they begged Him not to send them to the pit, which is locked right now. Thank God it is. We think things are bad today. During the tribulation, human suffering will be unimaginable.

In verses 3–11, we see the unleashing of the locusts.

> [3] Then out of the smoke, locusts came upon the earth. And to them was given power, as the scorpions of the earth have power. [4] They were commanded not to harm the grass of the earth, or any green thing, or any tree, but only those men who do not have the seal of God on their foreheads. [5] And they were not given authority to kill them, but to torment them for five months. Their torment was like the torment of a scorpion when it strikes a man. [6] In those days men will seek death and will not find it; they will desire to die, and death will flee from them.

Rather than eat grass, these locusts afflict people. Their lifespan is the lifespan of a natural locust, from May to September, fulfilling the prophecy of Joel Chapter 2.

> [7] The shape of the locusts was like horses prepared for battle. On their heads were crowns of something like gold, and their faces were like the faces of men. [8] They had hair like women's hair, and their teeth were like lions' teeth. [9] And they had breastplates like breastplates of iron, and the sound of their wings was like the sound of chariots with many horses running into battle. [10] They had tails like scorpions, and there were stings in their tails. Their power was to hurt men five months.

There we have their lifespan and a description of their mutated appearance. We might wonder where the script writers get their ideas for the gruesome creatures we see in horror movies. In verse 11, we learn that the leader of this band of demon locusts is Abaddon.

> [11] And they had a king over them the angel of the bottomless pit, whose name in Hebrew is Abaddon, but in Greek he has the name Apollyon.

This being is not Satan, but Abaddon, a leading fallen angel.

That's just one woe. There are two more to go.

Beginning in verse 12, we see the untying of the angels. That's just one woe. There are two more to go. Two more trumpet blasts. Two more woes.

> [12] One woe is past. Behold, still two more woes are coming after these things.

> [13] Then the sixth angel sounded: And I heard a voice from the four horns of the golden altar which is before God, [14] saying to the sixth angel who had the trumpet, "Release the four angels who are bound at the great river Euphrates." [15] So the four angels, who had been prepared for the hour and day and month and year, were released to kill a third of mankind. [16] Now the number of the army of the horsemen was two hundred million; I heard the number of them. [17] And thus I saw the horses in the vision: those who sat on them had breastplates of fiery red, hyacinth blue, and sulfur yellow; and the heads of the horses were like the heads of lions; and out of their mouths

came fire, smoke, and brimstone. [18] By these three
plagues, a third of mankind was killed – by the fire
and the smoke and the brimstone which came out
of their mouths. [19] For their power is in their mouth
and in their tails; for their tails are like serpents,
having heads; and with them they do harm.

These are fallen angels being released. Before earth time,
there was a rebellion in Heaven against God. Some angels were
cast out, becoming demons. In this sixth trumpet, we see these
fallen angels, these demons, being released. Although they are
evil, they will still accomplish the purpose of God. They are
bound to act within God's timetable, as verse 15 says.

Beginning in verse 16, we see the nature of this demonic
army. Some scholars speculate on this being an army of men.
Only China could possibly assemble a 200-million-man army
in the field today. Whatever the case, we know that one-third
of all humanity will die.

Suppose we have seven billion people in the world today.
That's the estimated number. Out of the 1.5 billion who *claim*
to be Christians, maybe one billion truly are. That would be
generous, but nevertheless, let's use that number to simplify
the math. That leaves six billion on the earth at the beginning
of the tribulation and one-third of them will die – two billion
people. The death of that many people is impossible to imagine.
It will be the most horrific, unbelievable event that has ever
happened on earth.

Next, we see how these people respond. In the midst of all
this, they still will not repent.

[20] But the rest of mankind, who were not killed by
these plagues, did not repent of the works of their
hands, that they should not worship demons, and

idols of gold, silver, brass, stone, and wood, which can neither see nor hear nor walk. ²¹ And they did not repent of their murders or their sorceries or their sexual immorality or their thefts.

Studying the original language of the Bible is helpful, but with our English translation of the Bible, we can compare Scriptures and still understand the truth of God's Word. Still, sometimes knowing what the original language says adds insight.

We get our English word *pharmacy* from the Greek word *pharmakeia*, which is translated as *sorcery* in verse 21. Drug use has reached an unbelievable acceptance in our culture. Just imagine what it's going to be like during the tribulation.

After a third of the world's inhabitants die, the people will still remain unrepentant in their hearts. They like their sin and want to stay in it.

Chapter 10

In Chapter 10, we find three intriguing scenes. The seven seals end with seven trumpets, and the last three trumpets are the woes.

Although the book of Revelation is an end-time book filled with symbolism, we should also give serious consideration to that which can be taken literally.

In the first verse of this chapter, an angel appears.

> [1] I saw still another mighty angel coming down from heaven, clothed with a cloud. And a rainbow was on his head, his face was like the sun, and his feet like pillars of fire. [2] He had a little book open in his hand. And he set his right foot on the sea and his left foot on the land, [3] and cried with a loud voice, as when a lion roars. When he cried out, seven thunders uttered their voices.

Most commentators agree that this angel is actually Jesus. Some would point out that Jesus is never specifically described as an angel in the book of Revelation, but He is mentioned numerous times in the Old Testament as the "angel of the

Lord." In Genesis 22, He called to Abraham. In Exodus 3, He was present with Moses. We also have references in Judges 2 and 2 Samuel 24.

Let's look at the angel and why we know He must be Jesus.

- He's clothed with a cloud. Matthews 17:5 speaks about Jesus' majesty.
- He is in a rainbow, and that divinity is seen in Revelation 4:3.
- His face is as the sun in brilliance in Revelation 1:16.
- He is described as having feet as fire, which is a judgment in Revelation 1:15.
- He has the voice of a lion, speaking with authority. Jeremiah 25:30 says the Lord will roar as a lion.

What a magnificent sight! With these attributes, this appearance may be none other than Jesus. He has one foot on the land, one on the sea, and He holds the book in His hand – the book that is the title deed to all humanity. He is the sovereign owner of it all.

We find an announcement coming from God beginning in verse 7.

> [4] Now when the seven thunders uttered their voices, I was about to write; but I heard a voice from heaven saying to me, "Seal up the things which the seven thunders uttered, and do not write them."
>
> [5] The angel whom I saw standing on the sea and on the land raised up his hand to heaven [6] and swore by Him who lives forever and ever, who created heaven and the things that are in it, the earth and the things that are in it, and the sea and the things that are in

it, that there should be delay no longer, [7] but in the days of the sounding of the seventh angel, when he is about to sound, the mystery of God would be finished, as He declared to His servants the prophets.

John is known as "the revelator," but here he assumes the role of "secret keeper." The messages given by the seven thunders are to be sealed. Only the people alive during the tribulation period will know what those words are. I'm glad I won't be here to find out but will learn about that when I'm in Heaven. The prophet Daniel says some information about future events "are closed up and sealed till the time of the end" (Daniel 12:9).

> *John is known as "the revelator," but here he assumes the role of "secret keeper."*

[8] Then the voice which I heard from heaven spoke to me again and said, "Go, take the little book which is open in the hand of the angel who stands on the sea and on the earth."

[9] So I went to the angel and said to him, "Give me the little book."

And he said to me, "Take and eat it; and it will make your stomach bitter, but it will be as sweet as honey in your mouth."

[10] Then I took the little book out of the angel's hand and ate it, and it was as sweet as honey in my mouth. But when I had eaten it, my stomach became bitter.

[11] And he said to me, "You must prophesy again
about many peoples, nations, tongues, and kings."

John ate the Word of God. It was sweet because the Word of
God is like honey from the honeycomb. It was bitter in John's
stomach because the judgments were painful.

Now we come to the place where the seventh angel is about
to sound and signify the end of the tribulation period.

Chapter 11

In concluding the seventh judgment and showing how the tribulation will end, Chapter 11 is essentially the beginning of the end.

In verse one, we learn about the temple.

> ¹ Then I was given a reed like a measuring rod. And the angel stood, saying, "Rise and measure the temple of God, the altar, and those who worship there."

At the time of John's writing this book, the temple Herod the Great had built was no longer standing. Many scholars believe John died somewhere around AD 90. Since the temple was destroyed in AD 70, much earlier than when he received the vision on the Isle of Patmos, we know the temple being measured here will be built during the tribulation.

Next, we are told about the times of the Gentiles.

> ² "But leave out the court which is outside the temple, and do not measure it, for it has been given to the Gentiles. And they will tread the holy city underfoot for forty-two months."

During this time of "forty-two months," the first three-and-a-half years during the tribulation, there will be a peace treaty between the Antichrist, Israel, and all the other nations. In the last three-and-a-half years, there will be wars and persecution of the Jewish people. The "times of the Gentiles" is a political term, referring to a period that began in 586 BC and will end when Jesus comes to rule and reign on this earth. From the time of the destruction of the first temple to Jesus' return to the earth as King, Gentiles will be the political power in the world order.

We read about two witnesses in verses 3 and 4.

> [3] "And I will give power to my two witnesses, and they will prophesy one thousand two hundred and sixty days, clothed in sackcloth."

> [4] These are the two olive trees and the two lamp-stands standing before the God of the earth.

Who are the witnesses? Israel is referred to as an olive tree. I think at least one of them is a Jew. Gentiles are seen as the candlesticks or the lampstands, but the text speaks of *two* individuals.

All types of speculation have risen about who these two men might be. Some think they are Enoch, who was translated into Heaven, and Elijah, who was carried up to Heaven. Since they didn't experience death on earth, the reasoning is that these men have to come back and die.

Others say the two witnesses had to be Enoch and Moses because of what the sixth verse says they have power to do. Personally, I believe it's just two indiscriminate, non-identified individuals. We don't know who these two witnesses will be, but we do know they will represent the Jew and the Gentile.

We see their testimony in verses 5–7.

⁵ And if anyone wants to harm them, fire proceeds from their mouth and devours their enemies. And if anyone wants to harm them, he must be killed in this manner. ⁶ These have power to shut heaven, so that no rain falls in the days of their prophecy; and they have power over waters to turn them to blood, and to strike the earth with all plagues, as often as they desire.

> *The witnesses are protected by God until their purpose is fulfilled.*

⁷ When they finish their testimony, the beast that ascends out of the bottomless pit will make war against them, overcome them, and kill them.

The witnesses are protected by God until their purpose is fulfilled. That's an important lesson for all of us. As one great preacher of yesteryear said, "I'm immortal in the will of God." As long as we're in the will of God, we can't be any safer.

As I've witnessed on the streets of Beirut, Lebanon, if God sends us to some dangerous place (like when I entered Shiite Muslim Hezbollah homes to tell them about Jesus), we are still safe in God's presence. We couldn't have been any safer there than if we were in our own living rooms, relaxing in a recliner.

If you're in the center of God's will, God has a purpose for your being where you are, and He will take care of you. As soon as His purpose for your life has been fulfilled, you have no more reason to remain on earth. You then belong with Christ in Heaven, where you will be eternally "at home."

We see terrorism at its worst in verse 8.

> [8] And their dead bodies will lie in the street of the
> great city which spiritually is called Sodom and
> Egypt, where also our Lord was crucified.

Where was Jesus crucified? In Jerusalem, outside the walls. The terrorists like to drag bodies into the street to strike fear in people's hearts and show themselves as victors. That's what they did in Mogadishu during a US military exercise. A helicopter was shot down. Some of our service personnel were killed. The enemy dragged the bodies of our heroes into the street as a sign of their victory and our defeat. The same thing happened in Baghdad. This is what terrorists do. The terrorists of the tribulation will be at it again.

Whether it's television or the Internet, as these events transpire, the terrible scenes will be viewed around the world.

> [9] Then those from the peoples, tribes, tongues,
> and nations will see their dead bodies three-and-
> a-half days, and not allow their dead bodies to be
> put into graves.

God will make a way for anyone and everyone to see the bodies of the prophets. They will be on all the network news channels. They will be the topic of daily conversation.

Next we see the attitude of the audience, as if they are celebrating in a coliseum after seeing people thrown to the lions. They are having a tailgate party and acting like it's a festive holiday.

> [10] And those who dwell on the earth will rejoice over
> them, make merry, and send gifts to one another,
> because these two prophets tormented those who
> dwell on the earth.

In verse 11, we see the tremendous power of God.

¹¹ Now after three-and-a-half days the breath of life
from God entered them, and they stood on their feet,
and great fear fell on those who saw them.

Resurrected from the dead, the two prophets are translated
to Heaven.

¹² And they heard a loud voice from heaven saying to
them, "Come up here." And they ascended to heaven
in a cloud, and their enemies saw them.

In the book of Genesis, we read about Enoch being translated.
"And Enoch walked with God; and he was not, for God took
him" (Genesis 5:24). Perhaps one day, he was walking toward
home when God said, "Enoch, why don't you come spend
the night with me," and Enoch went home with God. Since it
never becomes night in Heaven, Enoch never came back. One
day, the prophet Elijah was talking to Elisha when "suddenly
a chariot of fire appeared with horses of fire, and separated the
two of them; and Elijah went up by a whirlwind into heaven"
(2 Kings 2:11). After Jesus was raised from the dead, for forty
days on earth He showed Himself to be alive by many unde-
niable proofs and spoke to the people about the kingdom of
God. Then, "He was taken up, and a cloud received Him out
of their sight" (Acts 1:9).

The Bible records only those three who lived in their physical bodies when they were taken into Heaven. Believers will
experience this at the rapture.

In verse 13, a tenth of the city makes the evening news.

¹³ In the same hour there was a great earthquake,

and a tenth of the city fell. In the earthquake seven thousand people were killed, and the rest were afraid and gave glory to the God of heaven.

When seven thousand people die in an earthquake, we can be sure the tragedy will be breaking news on every channel. But the news will be coming two thousand years after it was first announced, because John wrote the headline scoop back in the first century.

> [14] The second woe is past. Behold, the third woe is coming quickly.

The last of the seven trumpets. The third and final woe. This finishes it up. This is where we find the conclusion of the tribulation and Jesus returning to earth to receive the kingdoms of this world to be His own.

> [15] Then the seventh angel sounded: And there were loud voices in heaven, saying, "The kingdoms of this world have become the kingdoms of our Lord and of His Christ, and He shall reign forever and ever!" [16] And the twenty-four elders who sat before God on their thrones fell on their faces and worshiped God, [17] saying:
>
>> "We give You thanks, O Lord God Almighty,
>> The One who is and who was and who is to come,
>> Because You have taken Your great power and reigned.
>> [18] The nations were angry, and Your wrath has come,
>> And the time of the dead, that they should be judged,

And that You should reward Your servants the
prophets and the saints,
And those who fear Your name, small and great,
And should destroy those who destroy the earth."

¹⁹ Then the temple of God was opened in heaven, and
the ark of His covenant was seen in His temple. And
there were lightnings, noises, thunderings, an earthquake, and great hail.

*We can have confidence
that one day, Jesus will
rule and reign.*

The last trumpet is being sounded.
Heaven is rejoicing at the justice of
God. The temple of God is seen with
the ark of God. This concludes the tribulation period and begins
the millennial reign of Christ.

The kingdoms of this earth will become the kingdoms of
our Lord.

We can have confidence that one day, Jesus will rule and reign.

Chapter 12

John's vision is now taking us back to review the tribulation and the Lord's judgment upon the earth. We begin with a description of the spiritual warfare in eternity past, which is still going on today and will continue through Chapter 18 with a retelling of the tribulation period. We'll see details about the Antichrist, the False Prophet, the one-world government, and the one-world religion.

In Chapter 12, we find four personages: Jesus, the Devil, Michael, and Israel. In verses 1, 2, 6, and 13–17, we see the woman mentioned in the Scriptures.

> [1] Now a great sign appeared in heaven: a woman clothed with the sun, with the moon under her feet, and on her head a garland of twelve stars. [2] Then being with child, she cried out in labor and pain to give birth.

In the sixth verse, we will learn that the woman had to "flee into the wilderness, where she has a place prepared by God, that they should feed her there one thousand two hundred and sixty days," or three-and-a-half years. Verses 13–17 tell us more about this mother, who symbolizes the nation of Israel. Joseph's dream of the sun, moon, and eleven stars (Genesis 37:9) gives a similar image of the nation of Israel. The prophets Isaiah and Jeremiah refer to Israel as a woman or as the wife of the Father (Isaiah 50:1; Jeremiah 3:1–25). The story of Hosea is the picture of redeeming love and how the Father is married to Israel (Hosea 2:1–23), just as Jesus is the bridegroom of the church. In a parable, Jesus likens Israel to a woman (Luke 18:1–8).

When we see this woman in verse six, we have a picture of Israel fleeing into the wilderness during the last half of the seven-year tribulation to a place prepared by God.

In the first three-and-a-half years, there is a false peace. The Antichrist makes a treaty, bringing what only appears to be peace to the nation of Israel and the world. But in the last half, the Jewish nation is severely persecuted. God miraculously supplies the needs of the Jews and saves them from annihilation in this place of protection. The prophet Daniel speaks of the land around Petra being protected from the wrath of the Antichrist (Daniel 11:41). Surely there is the possibility that the city of Petra might be the place where Israel will flee to safety.

In verses 3 and 4, we're given a vision of the monster who threatens the woman.

> [3] And another sign appeared in heaven: behold, a great, fiery red dragon having seven heads and ten horns, and seven diadems on his heads. [4] His tail drew a third of the stars of heaven and threw them to the earth. And the dragon stood before the woman who was ready to give birth, to devour her Child as soon as it was born.

Even before Eden, Satan had worked in opposition to God's will. No doubt, this dragon is the Devil. We will see in verse 9 that the serpent, the dragon, is the Devil.

The 7 heads are 7 world empires. The 7 crowns denote their full authority. Here we find Satan, once again, entering into conflict with the Creator, the God of our universe. The Devil is cast down a second time, and Jesus saw the Devil's first fall from Heaven.

Satan has had two times where he's come in direct conflict with God the Father. The first time, before time ever began, in eternity past, Satan was cast down. Then we find again during the time of the tribulation, he will be cast down.

Before we explore the difference in the two events, let's look at the Devil's origin. From the words of the prophet Ezekiel, we know the Devil was a created being (Ezekiel 28:12–19). The prophet Isaiah describes how pride rose in his heart, and this was the root of his iniquity

We live under the darkness of the ruler of darkness.

that brought his desire to ascend above the stars of God – above the other angels, above God Himself – and establish his throne of power over all (Isaiah 14:12–15). This was his first fall from Heaven. Yet he still has access to Heaven – sometimes described as "the prince and power of the air" (Ephesians 2:2). The apostle Paul refers to him as "the god of this world" (2 Corinthians 4:4).

If you wonder why we see so much evil around us and why there is so much hatred and violence against innocent people, it's because Satan is the god (little *g*) of this world. He controls the world system. Today we live in a sin-cursed environment. We live under the darkness of the ruler of darkness.

The Devil has access to Heaven today. This is the difference between the first and second falls of Satan. When he fell from Heaven the first time, he retained the right of entrance into God's presence so he could accuse the people. In this chapter, we will see that he's the "accuser of our brethren" (Revelation 12:10). Satan appeared before God's throne to accuse the perfect and upright Job, saying, "You have blessed the work of his hands, and his possessions have increased in the land. But now, stretch out Your hand and touch all that he has, and he will surely curse You to Your face!" (Job 1:10–11).

My wife, June, and I have two daughters. The oldest was fifteen when our son was born. When she was in college, he was going into kindergarten, so there was quite an age difference between our daughters and our son. When something would go wrong around the house, the girls would say, "Nathan did it," and he would say, "They are an accuser of the brethren." Perhaps his little ears had grasped a snippet of truth from my preaching. At any event, he understood what it was like to be accused and had connected it to Satan's role in Scripture.

The Devil is an accuser of the brethren. He goes before God and accuses the believer – and rightfully so in most cases. When we have failed to do the good we knew to do, we have sinned (James 4:17), and the Devil accuses us.

Thankfully, if you've been saved, you are under the blood of Jesus. The Devil's accusations have no power, because we have an advocate with the Father – Jesus Christ the righteous. He is our attorney in the highest court. Isn't it wonderful to know we have someone defending us in Heaven? He pleads our case when the accuser comes to the Father.

A third of the stars fell with the first casting down of Satan. We already know stars represent angels. A third of the angels joined the archangel Lucifer in his rebellion against God. They tried to usurp God's authority and were cast down to earth. When they fell in that rebellion, they became known as demons.

These fallen angels are spirit beings. We can't see them with our human eyesight, so there might be demons nearby right now. There definitely are demons at work across our land. More and more, I see human behavior around us suggests that demons are present in the United States, working behind the scene, encouraging evil. Demonic activity used to be less obvious, perhaps apparent in the wilds of the jungles of Africa or the Amazon River Basin. You might find idol worship in India or some far away region. But now we're seeing the influence of demons here in the United States.

Without a doubt, demons are present on earth. Jesus tells us about their activity and how they roam the earth (Matthew 12:43–45). The apostle Paul tells us they are in the air (Ephesians 2:2). Some are "reserved in everlasting chains under darkness" (Jude 1:6), in the bottomless pit (Revelation 9:1, 11). They are also in people (Mark 5:1–13). Demons are real, still active on earth.

As believers, we can be insulated from those demonic powers by the blood of Jesus.

In verse 4, we're reminded how Satan tried to stop the Messiah, seeking to kill the child the woman was bringing into this world. This is speaking of his attack upon Israel, not just upon Mary when Herod slew the boy babies in Bethlehem (Matthew 2:16). From the beginning, we see the Devil trying to kill the promised seed, as when Cain killed Abel. Twice the royal seed was reduced to one child. Satan tried to end the Jewish people through the persecutions of the Romans, the Nazis, and the communists in Stalinist Soviet Union. The Devil has always hated the Jewish people and the Jewish nation.

We see the second personage, the man child, in verse 5.

> ⁵ She bore a male Child who was to rule all nations with a rod of iron. And her Child was caught up to God and His throne.

> ⁶ Then the woman fled into the wilderness, where she has a place prepared by God, that they should feed her there one thousand two hundred and sixty days.

Without question, the male Child is Jesus, who rules with a

rod of iron (Revelation 2:27). The psalmist also says, "You shall break them with a rod of iron; You shall dash them to pieces like a potter's vessel" (Psalm 2:9). At His second coming, Jesus will take rightful control of the world order. No longer will Satan be the god of this world. Jesus will be the God of this world, with a capital G.

In the next verses, we see the archangel Michael leading an army against Satan.

> [7] And war broke out in heaven: Michael and his angels fought with the dragon; and the dragon and his angels fought, [8] but they did not prevail, nor was a place found for them in heaven any longer. [9] So the great dragon was cast out, that serpent of old, called the Devil and Satan, who deceives the whole world; he was cast to the earth, and his angels were cast out with him.

> [10] Then I heard a loud voice saying in heaven, "Now salvation, and strength, and the kingdom of our God, and the power of His Christ have come, for the accuser of our brethren, who accused them before our God day and night, has been cast down."

Here is that war in Heaven. This first casting out was positional. Satan lost his position in Heaven. The second casting out will be geographical. He will no longer have access to Heaven, to be able to appear before God's throne, or accuse the brethren.

The inhabitants of Heaven rejoiced at the removal of the adversary. This indicates that the events which take place on earth can be known by those in Heaven. Praise to Jesus erupts because of the victory over Satan.

The tribulation saints used three weapons of spiritual warfare against the adversary. You and I have the same weapons to use against demonic forces and Satan, although I seriously doubt whether I have ever ranked highly enough for Satan himself to be my direct adversary. A story is told that at the beginning of the Reformation period, Martin Luther had a confrontation with the Devil

> *Definitely, there are evil spirits, forces that work against us.*

and threw an inkwell at him. Don't worry about keeping an ink-well handy. That's not an effective weapon of spiritual warfare.

Looking back on my life, I believe I have experienced demonic attacks – times when Satanic forces wanted to stand against my ministry. Definitely, there are evil spirits, forces that work against us.

In verse 11, we are shown a secret weapon to use against Satan and his emissaries. Our power is not in magic words like *abracadabra*. It's not administered like some fairy dust you sprinkle. These three weapons exercise God's power through us, which is why we can use it in our spiritual warfare.

> [11] "And they overcame him by the blood of the Lamb and by the word of their testimony, and they did not love their lives to the death."

First of all, you have to be saved to have any chance at all in fighting the demonic foe.

Second, the Scripture says, "They overcame him by the word of their testimony," which is the Word of God. When Satan tempted Jesus in the wilderness (Luke 4:2–13), what did Jesus do? He quoted the Word of God back to Satan. The only way we can repel those demonic spirits who come against us is to use the word of the testimony of the Word of God.

The third weapon is crucial, which we see in the words, "They loved not their lives to the death." I believe this refers to our human will being totally submitted to the will of the Father. This goes so far as to declare unto God, "If you want me to live, I'll live by your help and grace," which is what the three Hebrew children said before they were thrown into the fiery furnace (Daniel 3:1–30). "We're not going to bow down to your idol, and if we die, we die. If God wants to deliver us, He'll deliver us."

The apostle Paul said, "I have been crucified with Christ; it is no longer I who live, but Christ lives in me; and the life which I now live in the flesh I live by faith in the Son of God, who loved me and gave Himself for me" (Galatians 2:20). A broken will, surrendered to the will of the Father.

While the heavens rejoice, the Devil is angry.

> ¹² "Therefore rejoice, O heavens, and you who dwell
> in them! Woe to the inhabitants of the earth and the
> sea! For the devil has come down to you, having great
> wrath, because he knows that he has a short time."

When Satan rebelled against God in the beginning, he was cast down positionally. Still with access to Heaven, he became the prince of the power of the air, the god of this world. He is relentless in his attempts to overthrow God's authority. He never learns.

We're going to see one last time when the Devil will do his very best to win. When he is cast down to earth, he will be literally pouring out his anger, doing all he can to take as many to Hell with him as he can.

Beginning in verse 13, we see the mother revisited, the representative of Israel, who is again fleeing to survive.

> ¹³ Now when the dragon saw that he had been cast to
> the earth, he persecuted the woman who gave birth

to the male Child. [14] But the woman was given two wings of a great eagle, that she might fly into the wilderness to her place, where she is nourished for a time and times and a half a time from the presence of the serpent. [15] So the serpent spewed water out of his mouth like a flood after the woman, that he might cause her to be carried away by the flood. [16] But the earth helped the woman, and the earth opened its mouth and swallowed up the flood which the dragon had spewed out of his mouth. [17] And the dragon was enraged with the woman, and he went to make war with the rest of her offspring, who keep the commandments of God and have the testimony of Jesus Christ.

The flood symbolizes a vast amount of water or a huge number of people who are coming against Israel. But for three-and-a-half years, God supplies her need. An earthquake swallows up the army. That's not the first time an earthquake has been used where the enemies of God have been swallowed. Satan continues until the last moment of the tribulation, trying to wipe out the Jews from the face of the earth. We see in verse 17 that he especially hates those who accept Jesus Christ as their Lord and Savior.

Chapter 13

In Chapter 13 we learn about the unholy trinity. Just as we know the Father, the Son, and the Holy Spirit as three persons, one God, so there are three personages which form the unholy trinity. You see, the Devil tries to copy everything God does. He's a mimicker.

Jesus had a victorious resurrection and lives today. During the tribulation, a man will be born who will appear as Satan incarnate. He will be killed and resurrected and will claim to be God. We know him as the Antichrist. In the Old Testament, he is known as the Assyrian (Isaiah 10, 30), King of Babylon (Isaiah 14), Lucifer (Isaiah 14), the Little Horn (Daniel 7–8), King of Fierce Countenance (Daniel 8), the Prince that shall come (Daniel Chapter 9), and Willful King (Daniel 11).

In the New Testament, we find him called the Antichrist (1 John 2), Man of Sin, the Son of Perdition, the Lawless One, and the Wicked One (2 Thessalonians 2).

Connecting all the end-time references in Daniel to what we have in the book of Revelation is an interesting study. We would soon realize that Daniel speaks even more of the Antichrist than what we find in the book of Revelation.

There are "many antichrists" (1 John 2:18), but there will be only one who is the Antichrist.

In this chapter, he's called the Beast.

> [1] Then I stood on the sand of the sea. And I saw a beast rising up out of the sea, having seven heads and ten horns, and on his horns ten crowns, and on his heads a blasphemous name. [2] Now the beast which I saw was like a leopard, his feet were like the feet of a bear, and his mouth like the mouth of a lion. The dragon gave him his power, his throne, and great authority.

Who is the dragon? The Devil. When Jesus was led by the Spirit to be tempted, Satan showed Him all the kingdoms of that world and said, "All these things I will give You if You will fall down and worship me" (Matthew 4:9). Well, the Antichrist is one who bowed down to Satan.

When Jesus told the Jews, "I have come in My Father's name, and you do not receive Me; if another comes in his own name, him you will receive" (John 5:43), He was making a prophetic reference to this Antichrist. Not only did Jesus predict His own suffering and that He would be "rejected by the elders and chief priests and scribes, and be killed" (Mark 8:31), but He said the Jews in particular, and the people of this earth in general, would welcome the Antichrist, gladly receiving him.

John saw this super-human figure having complete control of the earth just before Jesus returns to the earth. Four times, the word *power* is used, denoting an explosive capability, absolute authority, or total control. When the Devil makes his last attempt to keep the world under his sway, he uses the dynamic power of a charismatic superman, the Antichrist.

With his unrivaled power of leadership, the Antichrist will have the physical resources and diplomatic ability to rule the world. In Daniel, he is the beast who becomes king, "making war against the saints, and prevailing against them, until the Ancient of Days came, and a judgment was made in favor of the saints of the Most High, and the time came for the saints to possess the kingdom" (Daniel 7:21–22). He is Satan in human form with all the kingdoms of the world brought under his dominion.

We could be living in the last generation. There is some reason to believe we are.

In verses 3 and 4 we see the superman's power of life.

³ And I saw one of his heads as if it had been mortally wounded, and his deadly wound was healed. And all the world marveled and followed the beast.
⁴ So they worshiped the dragon who gave authority to the beast; and they worshiped the beast, saying, "Who is like the beast? Who is able to make war with him?"

When President John F. Kennedy was shot in the head, some people thought he must have been the Antichrist and expected him to rise from the dead. Of course, that didn't happen. Several years ago when the Pope was shot, some thought he was the Antichrist, even though the wound wasn't in the head. They seem to be looking for the powerful celebrity described in Scripture without realizing that when this happens, we won't be around to see it.

We could be living in the last generation. There is some reason to believe we are. In that case, the Antichrist could be alive today, but I doubt he has reached celebrity status. He's probably not someone we would point out, saying, "There is Satan's superman." That recognition will most likely come after the believers have been caught away to be with the Lord.

After rejecting Jesus' resurrection, the world will accept the resurrection of the Antichrist. Although God controls life and death, Satan has similar but inferior ability, and he is permitted to use it. Satan will give false experiences, manifesting his power to keep people from having a true experience of God and His power.

Jesus sometimes used sheep as a metaphor to describe God's people. Just as sheep are easily distracted and wander off, people are easily fooled by what looks real but isn't. You can have all kinds of experiences, but they are not necessarily valid evidence of God at work. Satan can be a miracle worker. Just remember that.

We see the Antichrist's power of language in verses 5 and 6.

> [5] And he was given a mouth speaking great things and blasphemies, and he was given authority to continue for forty-two months.

> [6] Then he opened his mouth in blasphemy against God, to blaspheme His name, His tabernacle, and those who dwell in heaven.

For three-and-a-half years, the Antichrist can say anything he wishes without being questioned. I think we see some forerunners of that in people today. Some politicians appear to be able to say whatever they want, and most of their constituents accept their messages without any interest in checking the facts. Their charismatic, persuasive language gives them power to command a large crowd of blind followers.

Satan's superman has the power to elicit loyalty, as we see in verses 7–10.

> [7] It was granted to him to make war with the saints and to overcome them. And authority was given him

over every tribe, tongue, and nation. ⁸ All who dwell
on the earth will worship him, whose names have
not been written in the Book of Life of the Lamb
slain from the foundation of the world.

⁹ If anyone has an ear, let him hear. ¹⁰ He who leads
into captivity shall go into captivity; he who kills
with the sword must be killed with the sword. Here
is the patience and the faith of the saints.

The Antichrist will demand complete obedience, as if every
knee must bow and every tongue must confess him to be lord.
People will receive his mark or be under the sentence of death.

Beginning in verse 11, we see the second person of the
unholy trinity. We have already seen Satan's superman who is
the Antichrist. Now we have Satan's super salesman, the False
Prophet.

¹¹ Then I saw another beast coming up out of the
earth, and he had two horns like a lamb and spoke
like a dragon.

Here we have a beast with horns. We're told in Daniel Chapter
7, the horns are kings, or those who are in authority. We will see
this beast referred to as the False Prophet in Revelation Chapters
16, 19, and 20. Jesus said, "False christs and false prophets will
rise and show great signs and wonders to deceive, if possible,
even the elect" (Matthew 24:24). His warning was about these
two who finally reach the pinnacle of power.

The image of a lamb speaking like a dragon tells us that the
False Prophet will appear to be meek, sincere, and truthful, but
his speech will be destructive. This is similar to an analogy Jesus

used. "Beware of false prophets, who come to you in sheep's clothing, but inwardly they are ravenous wolves" (Matthew 7:15).

Satan's super salesman appears in this description.

We see the deception of Satan's super salesman beginning in verse 12.

> [12] And he exercises all the authority of the first beast in his presence, and causes the earth and those who dwell in it to worship the first beast, whose deadly wound was healed. [13] He performs great signs, so that he even makes fire come down from heaven on the earth in the sight of men. [14] And he deceives those who dwell on the earth by those signs which he was granted to do in the sight of the beast, telling those who dwell on the earth to make an image to the beast who was wounded by the sword and lived. [15] He was granted power to give breath to the image of the beast, that the image of the beast should both speak and cause as many as would not worship the image of the beast to be killed. [16] He causes all, both small and great, rich and poor, free and slave, to receive a mark on their right hand or on their foreheads, [17] and that no one may buy or sell except one who has the mark or the name of the beast, or the number of his name.

> [18] Here is wisdom. Let him who has understanding calculate the number of the beast, for it is the number of a man: His number is 666.

The Devil is the great deceiver. Jesus described his nature, saying, "He was a murderer from the beginning, and does not stand in the truth, because there is no truth in him. When he speaks a lie, he speaks from his own resources, for he is a liar and the father of it" (John 8:44). Some people would often rather believe a lie than the truth. A miracle may not be all it appears to be – perhaps a display of power, a demonic manifestation. Believe the

Some people would often rather believe a lie than the truth.

Word of God above what you think you see. The Word of God is the filter through which we should pass all our experiences.

In verse 18, we see death by number. Those who don't receive the mark of the beast will be put to death. The number 666 is simply the number of humanity. Through the ages, people have tried to decipher what that number means. Some have said the number stands for a person, assigning it to various historical figures including Caesar, the Pope, Napoleon, Hitler, Stalin, Saddam Hussein, even US presidents such as John F. Kennedy, George W. Bush, or Barack Obama. After believers are caught away, God will reveal who the Antichrist is. Once that happens, to receive food or engage in commerce you must receive the mark of the beast.

The unholy trinity is comprised of the Devil (the dragon), the Antichrist, and the False Prophet.

Chapter 14

U p to this point, everything looks bleak, but some things are about to be made right. In this chapter, we find the power of God being demonstrated on the positive side. This is the turning of the tide, the assurance of victory for the believer, regardless of circumstances.

We see Mount Zion in Heaven in verses 1–5.

> ¹ Then I looked, and behold, a Lamb standing on Mount Zion, and with Him one hundred and forty-four thousand, having His Father's name written on their foreheads. ² And I heard a voice from heaven, like the voice of many waters, and like the voice of loud thunder. And I heard the sound of harpists playing their harps. ³ They sang as it were a new song before the throne, before the four living creatures, and the elders; and no one could learn that song except the hundred and forty-four thousand who were redeemed from the earth. ⁴ These are the ones who were not defiled with women, for they are virgins. These are the ones who follow the Lamb wherever He goes. These were redeemed from among men, being firstfruits to God and to the Lamb. ⁵ And

in their mouth was found no deceit, for they are
without fault before the throne of God.

Here is a worship scene in the literal place called Heaven,
including the 144,000 Jewish evangelists introduced back in
Chapter 7. This is God's abode, geographic and tangible. Those
who are saved from the tribulation are paid honor in Heaven.
Next, we see the messengers from Heaven.

> [6] Then I saw another angel flying in the midst of
> heaven, having the everlasting gospel to preach to
> those who dwell on the earth – to every nation, tribe,
> tongue, and people – [7] saying with a loud voice, "Fear
> God and give glory to Him, for the hour of His judg-
> ment has come; and worship Him who made heaven
> and earth, the sea and springs of water."

> [8] And another angel followed, saying, "Babylon is
> fallen, is fallen, that great city, because she has made
> all nations drink of the wine of the wrath of her
> fornication."

> [9] Then a third angel followed them, saying with a
> loud voice, "If anyone worships the beast and his
> image, and receives his mark on his forehead or
> on his hand, [10] he himself shall also drink of the
> wine of the wrath of God, which is poured out full
> strength into the cup of His indignation. He shall
> be tormented with fire and brimstone in the pres-
> ence of the holy angels and in the presence of the
> Lamb. [11] And the smoke of their torment ascends
> forever and ever; and they have no rest day or night,

who worship the beast and his image, and whoever receives the mark of his name."

¹² Here is the patience of the saints; here are those who keep the commandments of God and the faith of Jesus.

¹³ Then I heard a voice from heaven saying to me, "Write: 'Blessed are the dead who die in the Lord from now on.'"

"Yes," says the Spirit, "that they may rest from their labors, and their works follow them."

These angels delivered three messages. First of all, their message was about Jesus, with the angel circling the globe, preaching the Gospel. This is the only place in the Bible where we have an angel commissioned to preach the good news of Christ. All the nations will hear it – every people group, every language group, every ethnic group.

All the nations will hear it – every people group, every language group, every ethnic group.

Fallen angels have appeared on earth, bringing false gospels. Mohammed said an angel appeared to him. Joseph Smith said an angel appeared to him.

The apostle Paul issues a warning about angels bringing messages of untruth. "Even if we, or an angel from heaven, preach any other gospel to you than what we have preached to you, let him be accursed" (Galatians 1:8). He speaks of "false apostles, deceitful workers, transforming themselves into apostles of Christ. And no wonder! For Satan himself transforms himself into an angel of light. Therefore it is no great thing if his ministers also transform themselves into ministers of righteousness, whose end will be according to their works" (2 Corinthians 11:13–15).

For us in the church age, if we were to see Jesus standing at the foot of our bed, we had better pray that the blood of the real Lord Jesus Christ will cover us, because that's not Jesus. He's not at the foot of our bed, because we know He's in Heaven, at the right hand of the Father until the day when He arrives in the clouds in power and great glory to receive us to Himself. Any other apparition people might see could very well be a demonic spirit. Be careful about visions and so-called heavenly messengers.

The true messengers from Heaven, the angels we see in this chapter, not only brought the message of Jesus, but they brought the message of judgment and justice. We see the fall of the evil city Babylon with corresponding wrath falling on those who worship the beast.

Then the saints receive their just rewards to rest from their labors.

> [14] Then I looked, and behold, a white cloud, and on the cloud sat One like the Son of Man, having on His head a golden crown, and in His hand a sharp sickle. [15] And another angel came out of the temple, crying with a loud voice to Him who sat on the cloud, "Thrust in Your sickle and reap, for the time has come for You to reap, for the harvest of the earth is ripe." [16] So He who sat on the cloud thrust in His sickle on the earth, and the earth was reaped.
>
> [17] Then another angel came out of the temple which is in heaven, he also having a sharp sickle.
>
> [18] And another angel came out from the altar, who

had power over fire, and he cried with a loud cry to him who had the sharp sickle, saying, "Thrust in your sharp sickle and gather the clusters of the vine of the earth, for her grapes are fully ripe." [19] So the angel thrust his sickle into the earth and gathered the vine of the earth, and threw it into the great winepress of the wrath of God. [20] And the winepress was trampled outside the city, and blood came out of the winepress, up to the horses' bridles, for one thousand six hundred furlongs.

Jesus is the master of Heaven and earth. He is sovereign.

At the end of the tribulation, He will show His power as the reaper, described both here and in the Old Testament. "Put in the sickle, for the harvest is ripe. Come, go down; for the winepress is full, the vats overflow" (Joel 3:13).

This scene is in anticipation of Revelation Chapter 16:13–16, the consummation of the age when the great battle is fought. If the numbers are correct, we can calculate a river of blood flowing four feet deep for 175 miles, farther than from Megiddo to Jerusalem. Many dispute the possibility of the image being literal, but there are many incalculable occurrences which become realities during this tribulation time.

Chapter 15

Now we begin the seven last plagues. God permits evil to rule the world with unprecedented harshness. For seven years the wrath of God will be poured out. The last three-and-a-half years will be the greater part of the tribulation.

> [1] Then I saw another sign in heaven, great and marvelous: seven angels having the seven last plagues, for in them the wrath of God is complete.

In these judgments and the termination God's wrath, we see the Triumphant One.

> [2] And I saw something like a sea of glass mingled with fire, and those who have the victory over the beast, over his image and over his mark, and over the number of his name, standing on the sea of glass, having harps of God. [3] They sing the song of Moses, the servant of God, and the song of the Lamb, saying:
>
> "Great and marvelous are Your works,
> Lord God Almighty!
> Just and true are Your ways,

REVELATION: THE BEST IS YET TO COME

O King of the saints!
⁴ Who shall not fear You, O Lord, and glorify
Your name?
For You alone are holy.
For all nations shall come and worship before You,
For Your judgments have been manifested."

This is the same sea that was mentioned back in Revelation 4:6. The tribulation saints in Heaven are singing the song of the Jews, which is the song of Moses. They also sing the song of the redeemed, the song of the Lamb, which is the song of the Lord Jesus Christ. This indicates Jewish believers who have come out of the tribulation period, who are now in Heaven praising God. They have been martyred for Christ.

We see the temple in Heaven in verses 5–8.

⁵ After these things I looked, and behold, the temple of the tabernacle of the testimony in heaven was opened. ⁶ And out of the temple came the seven angels having the seven plagues, clothed in pure bright linen, and having their chests girded with golden bands. ⁷ Then one of the four living creatures gave to the seven angels seven golden bowls full of the wrath of God who lives forever and ever. ⁸ The temple was filled with smoke from the glory of God and from His power, and no one was able to enter the temple till the seven plagues of the seven angels were completed.

This is a literal worship center in Heaven. When Moses made the tabernacle, he followed a blueprint of what existed in Heaven (Hebrews 8:5; 9:23).

The tabernacle and temple of the Jews was patterned after

the worship center in Heaven. During the time of the fullness of the Gentiles, when non-Jews are the spiritual, religious leaders of this world, the church is the worship center.

One definition of the church is the mystical body of Christ, which includes all the people who have been saved. The Greek word *ekklesia*, meaning "a gathering of people," which we translate as "church,"

A person is no more the church than the temple.

appears 119 times in the New Testament. We're confident that 116 times, the word refers to a local assembly of believers.

The Bible plainly teaches that the worship center during this age is to be the New Testament church.

In His personal ministry, Jesus established the church. He implemented two church ordinances: (1) the Lord's Supper and (2) water baptism, which belong to the church collectively, not to individual believers. Sometimes I hear people say, "I'm the church." A person is no more the church than the temple. Believers are the temple of God, but not a literal temple. One person is not the literal church, because the church is a collective body of baptized believers who have banded themselves together to carry out The Great Commission.

The throne of mercy in Heaven becomes a throne of judgment. While we're here in the church age, let's realize that we have the responsibility of telling people the good news of Jesus Christ, because the day will come when they cannot and will not hear it.

Chapter 16

In this chapter, we see the angels in judgment, pouring out the bowls of wrath onto the earth. This is a judgment. Four of the seven bowls duplicate the plagues of Egypt, except that this time all the judgments cover the entire globe.

> ¹ Then I heard a loud voice from the temple saying to the seven angels, "Go and pour out the bowls of the wrath of God on the earth."

> ² So the first went and poured out his bowl upon the earth, and a foul and loathsome sore came upon the men who had the mark of the beast and those who worshiped his image.

The next bowl corresponds with the sixth Egyptian plague described in Exodus Chapter 9.

> ³ Then the second angel poured out his bowl on the sea, and it became blood as of a dead man; and every living creature in the sea died.

This sea could be the Mediterranean Sea, or it could be

referring to the earth's oceans. Even though we have a world-wide pouring out of the wrath of God, an individual judgment might focus on a particular region.

> [4] Then the third angel poured out his bowl on the rivers and springs of water, and they became blood. [5] And I head the angel of the waters saying:
>
>> "You are righteous, O Lord,
>> The One who is and who was and who is to be,
>> Because You have judged these things.
>> [6] For they have shed the blood of saints and prophets,
>> And You have given them blood to drink.
>> For it is their just due."
>
> [7] And I head another from the altar saying, "Even so, Lord God Almighty, true and righteous are Your judgments."

In this third bowl, judgment is brought upon those who have killed the believers, and the blood flows red like a river. Now they have blood to drink, which resembles the first Egyptian plague described in Exodus Chapter 7. The judgment is upon the fresh water, not the salt-water oceans. The ones who have rejected the grace of God will not have fresh water to drink.

In the fourth bowl, people who are in torment are still refusing to call out in mercy.

> [8] Then the fourth angel poured out his bowl on the sun, and power was given to him to scorch men with fire. [9] And men were scorched with great heat, and they blasphemed the name of God who has power over these plagues; and they did not repent and give Him glory.

The people have rebellious hearts during this horrible time. When trials, difficulties and afflictions come our way, we either run toward the Lord or we run in the opposite direction. We either get better or we get bitter. These people refuse to repent, unwilling to make any move toward God.

> [10] Then the fifth angel poured out his bowl on the throne of the beast, and his kingdom became full of darkness; and they gnawed their tongues because of the pain. [11] They blasphemed the God of heaven because of their pains and their sores, and did not repent of their deeds.

we either run toward the Lord or we run in the opposite direction.

In the fifth bowl, we see similarities to the ninth Egyptian plague, found in Exodus Chapter 10. We see that the bowl judgments overlap, because during this darkness they were still hurting from the sores.

The Euphrates River will dry up in the pouring out of the sixth bowl.

> [12] Then the sixth angel poured out his bowl on the great river Euphrates, and its water was dried up, so that the way of the kings from the east might be prepared. [13] And I saw three unclean spirits like frogs coming out of the mouth of the dragon, out of the mouth of the beast, and out of the mouth of the false prophet. [14] For they are spirits of demons, performing signs, which go out to the kings of the earth and of the whole world, to gather them to the battle of that great day of God Almighty.

> [15] "Behold, I am coming as a thief. Blessed is he who

watches, and keeps his garments, lest he walk naked and they see his shame."

[16] And they gathered them together to the place called in Hebrew, Armageddon.

The Jews in exile will be able to travel across that dry river-bed. Isaiah Chapter 11 tells us about that. With this event, we begin the preparation for the last great battle.

A thought of a final battle has always been in the human mind. People have always conceptualized good and evil finally coming to a cataclysmic point at the end of time. This is where good and evil battle. A bloody consummation is being prepared.

Where is the place of battle? Conservative scholars agree that the battle will begin in the Valley of Megiddo. We have *har*, meaning "mountain," and *megiddo*, meaning "destruction," or *Armageddon*. The hill of Megiddo is located west of the Jordan River, about ten miles south of Nazareth and fifteen miles from the Mediterranean coast.

This battle will begin and/or have its staging grounds at Megiddo and end in Jerusalem. Many Scriptures refer to the last day, but Ezekiel 38 gives details of how the battle is going to be arrayed, and many other aspects are found in Joel 3, Isaiah 34, Zechariah 14.

Who are the participants? The list of the nations who will participate is found in Ezekiel 38 – Russia, sub-Sahara Africans, Arabs, Turkey, Syria, Iran, Germany, Eastern European nations, and perhaps China are just some of the nations. Western Europe and their former colonies will be the revised Roman Empire. The Bible basically is silent about England and the United States.

The young lions described by Ezekiel pose a question to those who are coming against Israel: "Have you come to take plunder? Have you gathered your army to take booty, to carry away silver and gold, to take away livestock and goods, to take great plunder?" (Ezekiel 38:13). Speculation has it that this is the only possible presence of the United States and England. If true, then England and the United States either don't have the power or they lack the will to come to Israel's aid. I think our nation is rapidly moving in that direction today. No wonder we're not mentioned in prophecy.

> *The battle of Armageddon will take place all across Israel.*

The battle of Armageddon will take place all across Israel. Daniel Chapter 11 tells us Russia and her allies will come from the north. The Antichrist and the ten-nation confederacy will come from the west. Sub-Sahara Africans and the Arabs will move in from the south. China, or the "kings of the east," will come from the east (Revelation 16:12). Israel will be surrounded by the greatest armies of the world with no ally except one – Jesus. When Jesus is on your side, you're not going to lose.

What is the motivation for this convergence upon Israel? Various reasons are possible. The wealth of the nation, perhaps. Israel is a very wealthy nation. Rights to the resources of the land could be a factor. There's constant squabbling about land, and then there's the religious significance. The racial hatred of the Jews is demonically driven. No matter what all the factors are, the Antichrist's thirst for worship is probably the greatest driving force. He wants to be worshiped. The Jewish people have turned to the Messiah. Because of that, he wants them wiped out.

> [17] Then the seventh angel poured out his bowl into the air, and a loud voice came out of the temple of heaven, from the throne, saying, "It is done!" [18] And there were noises and thunderings and lightnings; and there was a great earthquake, such a mighty

and great earthquake as had not occurred since men were on the earth. [19] Now the great city was divided into three parts, and the cities of the nations fell. And great Babylon was remembered before God, to give her the cup of the wine of the fierceness of His wrath. [20] Then every island fled away, and the mountains were not found. [21] And great hail from heaven fell upon men, each hailstone about the weight of a talent. Men blasphemed God because of the plague of the hail, since that plague was exceedingly great.

God does not wink at sin. Right now, we live in an age of grace. Forgiveness awaits those who repent, but it won't always be that way.

The topography of the land is being reshaped. Islands and mountains will disappear. Babylon could be the city that houses the false religious system of the tribulation. Babylon could be referring to the sinful spiritual condition of Jerusalem. This event compares to the seventh plague in Egypt. "And Moses stretched out his rod toward heaven; and the Lord sent thunder and hail, and fire darted to the ground. And the Lord rained hail on the land of Egypt (Exodus 9:23).

A few years ago a hailstorm took place in the Dallas–Fort Worth Metroplex. A young man ran out to his truck to get his windows up. A hailstone hit him in the head and killed him. That hailstone wasn't any bigger than a softball, but it came down with such force it took his life. In the judgment time, much larger hailstones will be falling.

The blasphemers will be stoned, which is what the Bible says *should* happen to a blasphemer (Leviticus 24:16).

Many Scriptures throughout the Bible confirm the fact that these events will happen. Skeptics come and skeptics go, but the Word of God stands.

Chapter 17

All religions are not the same.

The Church of Satan in San Francisco was founded by Anton LaVey in 1966, which now reports to have about one million members.

In Chapter 17, we have what we might call the "Second Church of Satan."

> [1] Then one of the seven angels who had the seven bowls came and talked with me, saying to me, "Come, I will show you the judgment of the great harlot who sits on many waters, [2] with whom the kings of the earth committed fornication, and the inhabitants of the earth were made drunk with the wine of her fornication."

John reveals the rise and fall of the last false religious system that "sits on many waters," meaning a global multitude.

God sent a messenger to say His judgment is sure. Spiritual adultery is anything other than true worship of God. Pictured here is a powerful, populated, and prostituted church, in sharp contrast to the bride of Christ, who is pure and holy.

Next we see the identification of the harlot.

³ So he carried me away in the Spirit into the wilderness. And I saw a woman sitting on a scarlet beast which was full of names of blasphemy, having seven heads and ten horns. ⁴ The woman was arrayed in purple and scarlet, and adorned with gold and precious stones and pearls, having in her hand a golden cup full of abominations and the filthiness of her fornication. ⁵ And on her forehead a name was written:

> MYSTERY, BABYLON THE GREAT,
> THE MOTHER OF HARLOTS
> AND OF THE ABOMINATIONS
> OF THE EARTH.

⁶ I saw the woman, drunk with the blood of the saints and with the blood of the martyrs of Jesus. And when I saw her, I marveled with great amazement.

Now we see an explanation of this false religious system.

⁷ But the angel said to me, "Why did you marvel? I will tell you the mystery of the woman and of the beast that carries her, which has the seven heads and the ten horns. ⁸ The beast that you saw was, and is not, and will ascend out of the bottomless pit and go to perdition. And those who dwell on the earth will marvel, whose names are not written in the Book of Life from the foundation of the world, when they see the beast that was, and is not, and yet is. ⁹ Here is the mind which has wisdom: The seven heads are seven mountains on which the woman sits."

I know of only one Christian religious system that could meet all this description, a system that had its beginning around AD 300 and continues to this present hour. Only God knows what it will become in future years with its scarlet-colored clothing, great wealth, and a golden cup in its worship. Rome is famously called "the city of seven hills."

The false church of the end time is not necessarily the organization that exists today. During the tribulation, it will become the Antichrist church. We know it will be different in some ways, because the false church of the tribulation will incorporate all other religious systems.

the false church of the tribulation will incorporate all other religious systems.

[10] "There are also seven kings. Five have fallen, one is, and the other has not yet come. And when he comes, he must continue a short time. [11] The beast that was, and is not, is himself also the eighth, and is of the seven, and is going to perdition.

[12] "The ten horns which you saw are ten kings who have received no kingdom as yet, but they receive authority for one hour as kings with the beast. [13] These are of one mind, and they will give their power and authority to the beast. [14] These will make war with the lamb, and the Lamb will overcome them, for He is Lord of lords and King of kings; and those who are with him are called, chosen, and faithful."

[15] Then he said to me, "The waters which you saw, where the harlot sits, are peoples, multitudes, nations, and tongues. [16] And the ten horns which you saw on the beast, these will hate the harlot, make her

desolate and naked, eat her flesh and burn her with fire. [17] For God has put it into their hearts to fulfill His purpose, to be of one mind, and to give their kingdom to the beast, until the words of God are fulfilled. [18] And the woman whom you saw is that great city which reigns over the kings of the earth."

It is a religious system. Unsaved people will be fooled by the Antichrist and his religious system. The Antichrist will head the organization that rules the people, both politically and religiously. He will gain his control through his imitation of Jesus' death and resurrection. Many will worship him.

Before Jesus returns, the Antichrist and his forces will build a globally powerful religious system. But when Jesus comes, the Antichrist and his vast false religion will be brought down.

God works in the minds of evil people to produce good for us and to bring glory to Himself. Satan, the Antichrist, and the False Prophet – all with limited power – are seen here fulfilling God's purpose. We should not be surprised at this, because God is the One who is sovereign.

Our Lord Jesus Christ is King of kings and Lord of lords. He will win in the end.

Chapter 18

In this chapter, the tribulation period is coming to a close. In review, we remember the unholy trinity – the Antichrist, the False Prophet, and the dragon, who is the Devil himself. In the last chapter, we saw these unholy three and their system of religion that brings all the world churches together with a one-world government. The world will have one ruler: the Antichrist, who dies from a head wound and is resurrected, mimicking Jesus. After rejecting our resurrected Lord, the world will accept the resurrected Antichrist.

At the end of the tribulation, the political system run by the Antichrist turns against the religious system that is perpetuating worship of the Antichrist.

We will again see the harlot woman, first mentioned in the last chapter, who at first had preeminence over the Antichrist. But now the Antichrist and the ten-nation confederacy turns on her and this religious system. She is called a city. She is destroyed.

First we see the angelic indictment.

> ¹ After these things I saw another angel coming
> down from heaven, having great authority, and
> the earth was illuminated with his glory. ² And he

cried mightily with a loud voice, saying, "Babylon
the great is fallen, is fallen, and has become a
dwelling place of demons, a prison for every foul
spirit, and a cage for every unclean and hated bird!
³ For all the nations have drunk of the wine of the
wrath of her fornication, the kings of the earth
have committed fornication with her, and the merchants of the earth have become rich through the
abundance of her luxury."

This was a marriage between the state and the church,
which always results in disaster. The demons are behind the
false doctrine and the denial of biblical truth.

Next, we hear the announcement.

⁴ And I heard another voice from heaven saying,
"Come out of her, my people, lest you share in her
sins, and lest you receive of her plagues."

As strange as it may seem, there will be some who have
escaped the mark of the beast. Without the mark, they have
somehow survived in this false religious system. These survi-
vors are now being called out.

Then we have the appropriate indignation.

⁵ "For her sins have reached to heaven, and God has
remembered her iniquities. ⁶ Render to her just as she
rendered to you, and repay her double according to
her works; in the cup which she has mixed, mix double for her. ⁷ In the measure that she glorified herself
and lived luxuriously, in the same measure give her
torment and sorrow; for she says in her heart, 'I sit as
queen, and am no widow, and will not see sorrow.' ⁸

Therefore her plagues will come in one day – death and mourning and famine. And she will be utterly burned with fire, for strong is the Lord God who judges her.

⁹ "The kings of the earth who committed fornication and lived luxuriously with her will weep and lament for her, when they see the smoke of her burning, ¹⁰ standing at a distance for fear of her torment, saying, 'Alas, alas, that great city Babylon, that mighty city! For in one hour your judgment has come.'

The false religious system will be judged and punished in accordance with the pain and suffering, the great persecution, that it has inflicted upon the people. Those who enjoy evil will suffer accordingly. This judgment will happen quickly.

When speaking of the kings of the earth committing fornication, verse 9 is talking about spiritual adultery. In the worship of the Antichrist, the church and the state have engaged in spiritual adultery. This judgment on the false religious system is appropriate indignation because of the great persecution inflicted upon believers, who were martyred for the name of Jesus.

Those who enjoy evil will suffer accordingly.

In the next verses, we see the anguished investors.

¹¹ "And the merchants of the earth will weep and mourn over her, for no one buys their merchandise any more: ¹² merchandise of gold and silver, precious stones and pearls, fine linen and purple, silk and scarlet, every kind of citron wood, every kind of object of ivory, every kind of object of most precious wood, bronze, iron, and marble; ¹³ and cinnamon

and incense, fragrant oil and frankincense, wine and oil, fine flour and wheat, cattle and sheep, horses and chariots, and bodies and souls of men. [14] The fruit that your soul longed for has gone from you, and all the things which are rich and splendid have gone from you, and you shall find them no more at all. [15] The merchants of these things, who became rich by her, will stand at a distance for fear of her torment, weeping and wailing, [16] and saying, 'Alas, alas, that great city that was clothed in fine linen, purple, and scarlet, and adorned with gold and precious stones and pearls! [17] For in one hour such great riches came to nothing.' Every shipmaster, all who travel by ship, sailors, and as many as trade on the sea, stood at a distance [18] and cried out when they saw the smoke of her burning, saying, 'What is like this great city?'

> *Without warning, in an instant, everything is lost.*

[19] "They threw dust on their heads and cried out, weeping and wailing, and saying, 'Alas, alas, that great city, in which all who had ships on the sea became rich by her wealth! For in one hour she is made desolate.'

The world economy collapses with the fall of this false system. Without warning, in an instant, everything is lost. The profiteers weep because there is no hope of recovery.

In 1929, when the US stock market collapsed, people literally leaped out the windows of high-rise buildings, taking their lives because they had lost their fortunes. Millions of people stood in bread lines because there were no jobs and no money. They had to depend on government goodwill to receive something to eat. Those were desperate and terrible times.

Some people remember the recession of 2008. They may talk about economic hardships, how prices keep going up, how difficult it is to find a job. Those problems are nowhere close to being as severe as the Great Depression in 1929.

In this chapter, we're seeing an economic crash that is more catastrophic than we could ever imagine – profoundly worse than had ever been experienced before. Suddenly, the rich have nothing, because their money is worthless. Gold, silver, and diamonds become worthless when all you have isn't enough to buy food.

The avenged injustices come next.

> [20] "Rejoice over her, O heaven, and you holy apostles and prophets, for God has avenged you on her!"

> [21] Then a mighty angel took up a stone like a great millstone and threw it into the sea, saying, "Thus with violence the great city Babylon shall be thrown down, and shall not be found anymore. [22] The sound of harpists, musicians, flutists, and trumpeters shall not be heard in you anymore. No craftsman of any craft shall be found in you anymore, and the sound of a millstone shall not be heard in you anymore. [23] The light of a lamp shall not shine in you anymore, and the voice of bridegroom and bride shall not be heard in you anymore. For your merchants were the great men of the earth, for by your sorcery all the nations were deceived. [24] And in her was found the blood of prophets and saints, and of all who were slain on the earth."

Utter destruction comes upon this false system. From earlier in our study, you may remember the word translated "sorcery." In the original text, we have the Greek word *pharmakeia*, which means "drug use," "enchantments," "spells," or "potions." If we think about how many dependencies our society has today – alcohol, amphetamines, marijuana, prescription drugs, cocaine – the list is endless. We can easily see how drugs might be used to control the masses. Obviously, that will be a part of this false religious system.

God will avenge the blood of His prophets and saints. All those who have been part of that false religious system from the rising of the Tower of Babel to the fall of Babylon will experience God's vengeance. The *Babylon* described here is not the literal city of Babylon but the false religious system of the world, which has been the persecutor of the redeemed throughout the ages.

In one hour, God will avenge the blood of the righteous, and all the injustices will be set right. God will balance the books.

Chapter 19

We now come to the second phase of the second coming of Christ. After being caught up in all the turmoil of the tribulation, we still need to remember the trumpet judgments. The seals have been broken. The trumpets have sounded. The woes have been heard, the bowls of wrath poured out. All these things have been happening during those seven years.

People have received the mark of the beast on their hands or foreheads. The plagues, similar to what came upon Egypt in the days of Moses, have come again, but this time in greater measure around the globe. There's the Antichrist, the False Prophet, and the trauma of the Jewish people. One-third of all the people living on the face of the earth have died. The tragedy of the tribulation is worse than words can describe.

But at the same time, we're in Heaven. We're the redeemed. We're at the judgment seat of Christ, praising Jesus, casting our crowns at His feet. We're at the marriage supper of the Lamb.

Something new is about to happen on earth. Jesus is going to come with His saints. Exactly as He promised, He will return.

In this chapter, we see the majesty of Heaven's reaction to the judgment on Babylon. Praise is offered to God. Four hallelujahs are given.

First comes a praise for regeneration.

¹ After these things I heard a loud voice of a great multitude in heaven, saying, "Alleluia! Salvation and glory and honor and power belong to the Lord our God!

Next we see a praise for righteousness.

² "For true and righteous are His judgments, because He has judged the great harlot who corrupted the earth with her fornication; and He has avenged on her the blood of His servants shed by her." ³ Again they said, "Alleluia! Her smoke rises up forever and ever!"

After that, a hallelujah for the rightful one.

⁴ And the twenty-four elders and the four living creatures fell down and worshiped God who sat on the throne, saying, "Amen! Alleluia!" ⁵ Then a voice came from the throne, saying, "Praise our God, all you His servants and those who fear Him, both small and great!"

And finally our praise of restoration.

⁶ And I heard, as it were, the voice of a great multitude, as the sound of many waters and as the sound of mighty thunderings, saying, "Alleluia! For the Lord God Omnipotent reigns!"

The kingdom of Heaven is coming to earth, and there is a hallelujah time.

In verses 7–21, three meals are mentioned. We want to

participate in two of those meals, but of one we cannot and should not and would not participate. We don't want to be the main course at that meal because that will be a meal of those who are coming against the people of God. In that meal, the enemies of God will be consumed. The birds of the air will eat their carcasses.

We begin with the marriage supper, a meal that all of us want to be part of.

> *We don't want to be the main course at that meal because that will be a meal of those who are coming against the people of God.*

[7] "Let us be glad and rejoice and give Him glory, for the marriage of the Lamb has come, and His wife has made herself ready." [8] And to her it was granted to be arrayed in fine linen, clean and bright, for the fine linen is the righteous acts of the saints.

[9] Then he said to me, "Write: 'Blessed are those who are called to the marriage supper of the Lamb!'" And he said to me, "These are the true sayings of God." [10] And I fell at his feet to worship him. But he said to me, "See that you do not do that! I am your fellow servant, and of your brethren who have the testimony of Jesus. Worship God! For the testimony of Jesus is the spirit of prophecy."

The marriage supper of the Lamb makes a wonderful study on its own. John the Baptist alludes to the greatest celebration banquet of all time and eternity, saying, "You yourselves bear me witness, that I said, 'I am not the Christ,' but, 'I have been sent before Him.' He who has the bride is the bridegroom; but the friend of the bridegroom, who stands and hears him, rejoices greatly because of the bridegroom's voice. Therefore this joy of mine is fulfilled" (John 3:28–29).

There will be guests. There will be servants. There will be the bride and the bridegroom. The family of God will be present. It will be a wonderful time.

Jesus is the bridegroom, the central figure.

In our western culture, the bridegroom stands beside the preacher and eagerly waits for the music that announces the moment when his beautiful bride will come down the aisle. Everyone stands and turns to look at her. In our western culture, the bride is the one who receives the greatest honor. I'm sorry, ladies, but that's not the way it is in the eastern culture where the spotlight is on the groom.

In the marriage supper of the Lamb, our focus will be on the bridegroom – the Lord Jesus Christ. He gets the attention.

The bride, who is the church, has made herself ready. Some might say it's a faithful bride, and others who are saved are not part of the bride but will simply be there as guests or servants. It really doesn't matter, because what we know for sure is that all the redeemed are invited. We all get to join the festivities at the marriage supper of the Lamb.

What comes after the marriage supper? As we might expect, we have the honeymoon. Jesus will bring His bride back to earth for a one-thousand-year jubilee.

What an exciting time it will be when we return to earth with Jesus.

In verse 11, we come to the second supper.

> [11] Now I saw heaven opened, and behold, a white horse. And He who sat on him was called Faithful and True, and in righteousness He judges and makes war. [12] His eyes were like a flame of fire, and on His head were many crowns. He had a name written that

no one knew except Himself. [13] He was clothed with a robe dipped in blood, and His name is called The Word of God. [14] And the armies in heaven, clothed in fine linen, white and clean, followed Him on white horses. [15] Now out of His mouth goes a sharp sword, that with it He should strike the nations. And He Himself will rule them with a rod of iron. He Himself treads the winepress of the fierceness and wrath of Almighty God. [16] And He has on His robe and on His thigh a name written:

Is there anything else? Yes, we anticipate His soon return.

KING OF KINGS AND LORD OF LORDS.

Most churches observe the Lord's Supper – what we call the Eucharist, "the memorial supper," or simply "communion" – the ordinance of partaking of the bread and the fruit of the vine in obedience to what Jesus told His disciples at His last Passover supper. He took the bread, gave thanks, broke it, and then gave it to His disciples, saying, "This is My body which is given for you; do this in remembrance of Me" (Luke 22:19). When we partake of the memorial supper, not only are we reminded of what Jesus has done for us, but we remember that He died, was raised from the dead, and ascended into Heaven. Is there anything else? Yes, we anticipate His soon return. He is coming again.

Referring to the Lord's Supper, the apostle Paul said, "For as often as you eat this bread and drink this cup, you proclaim the Lord's death till He comes" (1 Corinthians 11:26). This passage points to the certain, sovereign return of Jesus. So when we observe the Lord's Supper, an important part of our remembrance is that Jesus is coming again. Hallelujah! He shed His blood to pay for our sins, and He is coming again.

In verses 17–21 we are given a glimpse of the Macabre Supper, extremely strange and very horrific.

> [17] Then I saw an angel standing in the sun; and he cried with a loud voice, saying to all the birds that fly in the midst of heaven, "Come and gather together for the supper of the great God [18] that you may eat the flesh of kings, the flesh of captains, the flesh of mighty men, the flesh of horses and of those who sit on them, and the flesh of all people, free and slave, both small and great."

> [19] And I saw the beast, the kings of the earth, and their armies, gathered together to make war against Him who sat on the horse and against His army. [20] Then the beast was captured, and with him the false prophet…

Now we see the Antichrist and the False Prophet.

> …who worked signs in his presence, by which he deceived those who received the mark of the beast and those who worshiped his image. These two were cast alive into the lake of fire burning with brimstone. [21] And the rest were killed with the sword which proceeded from the mouth of Him who sat on the horse. And all the birds were filled with their flesh.

What a terrifying event. In the jubilation for the redeemed, we see the judgment for the unredeemed, the literal carnage of the battle of Armageddon.

We have studied about the armies of the world coming in from all directions. Perhaps it will be a 200-million-man Chinese army that will come from the east. We do know there will be a huge army coming from that direction. Coming from the north, we have Russia and its sister nations. From the west, the ten-nation confederacy, and from the south, the Arab nations and the sub-Saharan Africans. All of them will be coming.

All these military forces of the world will join to move against that tiny country known as Israel, motivated to eliminate the Jewish problem. They have "the final solution," as Adolf Hitler called it, to annihilate the Jewish people. Israel has no hope.

We see no US military present. The United States either lacks the will or the ability to defend Israel against so great an army.

What will happen to the Jews? Unless Jesus appears, they will be utterly destroyed. Jesus does exactly that, arriving just in time with His army of saints. This is a supernatural, spiritual army. With the power of His mouth, Jesus spoke the world into existence, and He will, with words, destroy the armies that are coming against Israel.

The number of dead is so great, seven months will be needed to bury them (Ezekiel 39:12), and during that time the birds of the air are having a macabre feast. The supper of death. There will be a literal cleansing of the land by the birds of the air. It's a gruesome day – the day of the Lord. Judgment has finally come to those who have rejected the true and living God.

When Jesus returns, He will defeat all the armies that have come against Israel. Blood will be flowing like a river, its depth up to the horse's bridle – four feet deep and 175 miles long. It will be a more ghastly, horrific, heinous scene than anyone could imagine. No video game, no sci-fi movie, no tale of horror could ever capture the images of the judgment that will come upon those nations.

When Jesus comes with His army of saints, He will judge the nations and separate the righteous from the unrighteous like a shepherd divides sheep from goats. We see a description of that in Matthew 25:31–46. To some, He will say, "Come, you blessed of My Father, inherit the kingdom prepared for you from the foundation of the world," but to others He will say, "Depart from Me, you cursed, into the everlasting fire prepared for the Devil and his angels." Some will go into everlasting punishment, but the righteous will enjoy eternal life.

Chapter 20

In John's vision, we now come to the thousand-year period, which is the climax of the whole drama of the ages. The battle called Armageddon is over. Jesus now returns to earth to rule and reign for a thousand years.

John the Revelator records the final events of this world as we know it. Because we know how this story ends for us, we Christians can have confidence today, knowing that our present pain and suffering, our tests and trials, our fears and frustrations are nothing compared to the glories that lie ahead. The apostle Paul said, "The sufferings of this present time are not worthy to be compared with the glory which shall be revealed in us" (Romans 8:18). Even now, we can celebrate, because we know God is moving us toward the final victory.

In verses 1–10, we see the first of two main topics in this chapter: the Golden Age.

> ¹ Then I saw an angel coming down from heaven, having the key to the bottomless pit and a great chain in his hand. ² He laid hold of the dragon, that serpent of old, who is the Devil and Satan, and bound him for a thousand years; ³ and he cast him into the bottomless pit, and shut him up, and set a

seal on him, so that he should deceive the nations no more till the thousand years were finished. But after these things he must be released for a little while.

⁴ And I saw thrones, and they sat on them, and judgment was committed to them. Then I saw the souls of those who had been beheaded for their witness to Jesus and for the word of God, who had not worshiped the beast or his image, and had not received his mark on their foreheads or on their hands. And they lived and reigned with Christ for a thousand years. ⁵ But the rest of the dead did not live again until the thousand years were finished. This is the first resurrection. ⁶ Blessed and holy is he who has part in the first resurrection. Over such second death has no power, but they shall be priests of God and of Christ, and shall reign with Him a thousand years.

Jesus – He is the rightful King. The angel Gabriel said to Mary, "You will conceive in your womb and bring forth a Son, and shall call His name Jesus. He will be great, and will be called the Son of the Highest; and the Lord God will give Him the throne of His father David" (Luke 1:31–32). His birth was fulfilled two thousand years ago, and now He comes to reign.

After Jesus was arrested, what did He say to Pilate? "My kingdom is not of this world" (John 18:36). The first time He came to earth, He had a cross to bear, coming as the suffering servant, fulfilling the prophecy of Isaiah 53. He came to die for our sins, to forgive us. He came to make us victors instead of victims in the righteous judgment of a holy God. But this time, in the second coming, Jesus will fulfill Gabriel's promise. He will sit on the throne of David to reign for a thousand years.

Jesus will be King over all the earth, reigning from Jerusalem (Zechariah 14:8–9). The earth will return to its Edenic beauty. "The mountains and the hills shall break forth into singing before you, and all the trees of the field shall clap their hands. Instead of the thorn shall come up the cypress tree, and instead of the brier shall come up the myrtle tree" (Isaiah 55:12–13). There will be bounty in crops and wildlife. "The desert

The land will look like it did in the garden of Eden before Adam and Eve sinned.

shall rejoice and blossom as the rose" (Isaiah 35:1). Longevity of human life will be like it was before the flood. Peace will be evident in the animal kingdom.

It will be a golden age. The land will look like it did in the garden of Eden before Adam and Eve sinned.

We should recognize one remarkable feature about this thousand-year reign: Satan will be bound.

For all the time that we've been a part of this world, Satan has been its god (2 Corinthians 4:4). We wonder how people can commit such atrocities, how ruthless dictators can order the slaughter of millions of innocent people, how injustices can seem right to unjust judges and juries. How can people lie, cheat, and steal and believe their only wrong is in being caught? For those of us who have learned to love our neighbors and do good to those who would harm us, it's difficult to understand the evil forces that rule this world. We live in a sin-cursed society because Satan has its oversight, where he and his demons are still influencing what people think and do.

Powerful as Satan may be, he is not omnipotent.

God has power over all, including power over Satan and his demons. The knowledge, wisdom, and power of God stand supreme above all that He has created. He alone is all-powerful.

Satan is the god of this world for only as long as God allows him to continue. Yes, Satan is behind many of the things that happen, but God is also at work behind the scenes.

The day will come when Satan will be bound. An angel will bind him with chains for a thousand years (Revelation 20:2). He will be cast into the bottomless pit, imprisoned there.

When Jesus begins His reign, the saints will rule with him. Jesus said, "When the Son of Man sits on the throne of His glory, you who have followed Me will also sit on twelve thrones, judging the twelve tribes of Israel" (Matthew 19:28). Some have found significance in the parable where Jesus said, "Because you were faithful in a very little, have authority over ten cities" (Luke 19:17). Who knows? A pastor may come back as the mayor of a city. Wouldn't that be something? We don't know how it's going to happen. We don't know where our positions will be. We do know we will be given assignments, because there has to be work involved if we have a part in reigning with him. For a thousand years, we will live on earth in glorified bodies, like the body Jesus had when He rose from the grave.

We don't know much about what these glorified bodies will be like. Evidently, if we're going to live on earth a thousand years, our bodies don't grow old. A thousand years is longer than Methuselah lived. We know that Jesus ate fish and honeycomb after the resurrection (Luke 24:41–42), so I'm thinking we may not have to watch our diets so much. We'll live in perfect health. Exercise is something we will do to serve the Lord, not to avoid becoming obese.

Now let's see what happens after the millennium.

> [7] Now when the thousand years have expired, Satan will be released from his prison [8] and will go out to deceive the nations which are in the four corners of the earth, Gog and Magog, to gather them together to battle, whose number is as the sand of the sea. [9]

They went up on the breadth of the earth and surrounded the camp of the saints and the beloved city.
And fire came down from God out of heaven and
devoured them. ¹⁰ The devil, who deceived them,
was cast into the lake of fire and brimstone where
the beast and the false prophet are. And they will be
tormented day and night forever and ever.

After a thousand years in chains, Satan will be released for
one purpose: to deceive those who can be deceived. Those who
came through the tribulation will have children. Some will be
deceived. They will believe a lie and will follow Satan.

This is beyond my understanding, how people could live for
a thousand years with Christ and still be vulnerable to Satan's
deception. Sinners will still rebel, a most amazing thing.

Peace will prevail. Jesus and the saints who rule with Him
would never allow sin to run rampant on this earth. Even so,
some people will still rebel.

We need to recognize our vulnerability so we never let
go of our trust and dependence upon Christ. Without Him
working in our lives, "the heart is deceitful above all things,
and desperately wicked" (Jeremiah 17:9). We think we know
ourselves. I've heard people say, "Oh, I would never do that."
And later I've seen them caught in that very sin.

Apart from God, I'm capable of doing anything evil and
sinful and so are you. It's only by the grace of God that we can
live a pure and holy life. When we trust our own self-discipline
and think we have the willpower to avoid sin, we're only fooling ourselves. We are forever dependent upon the power of the
Holy Spirit to live holy lives, pleasing to our Heavenly Father.

We've seen the rebellion of sinners before, and we will see it
again at the end of the millennium. Satan led the first rebellion
in eternity past, when he took a third of the angels with him. In

John's vision, we have seen him lead a second rebellion at the beginning of the tribulation. Now, he will lead a third rebellion at the end of the thousand-year reign of Christ.

God is omnipotent. Satan's defeat is guaranteed. As it says in verse 10, he will be cast into "the Lake of Fire and brimstone" where the beast (the Antichrist) and the False Prophet are. "They will be tormented day and night forever and ever." Since the Antichrist and the False Prophet have been there for a thousand years, it is apparent that punishment in the Lake of Fire is eternal not annihilation.

Hallelujah! Finally, we're rid of the Devil.

I am so thankful we know we win in the end.

We now move to the next topic of this chapter: the Great White Throne.

> [11] Then I saw a great white throne and Him who sat on it, from whose face the earth and the heaven fled away. And there was found no place for them. [12] And I saw the dead, small and great, standing before God, and books were opened. And another book was opened, which is the Book of Life. And the dead were judged according to their works, by the things which were written in the books. [13] The sea gave up the dead who were in it, and Death and Hades delivered up the dead who were in them. And they were judged, each one according to his works. [14] Then Death and Hades were cast into the lake of fire. This is the second death. [15] And anyone not found written in the Book of Life was cast into the lake of fire.

The throne is the center of activity in these last moments of earth's current existence.

Jesus sits as judge on the throne. "For the Father judges no one, but has committed all judgment to the Son" (John 5:22). The Word of God is the basis for this judgment. Jesus said, "He who rejects Me, and does not receive My words, has that which judges him – the word that I have spoken will judge him in the last day" (John 12:48). In His infinite knowledge and wisdom, every work will be judged, and He will make no mistakes. "For God will bring every work into judgment, including every secret thing, whether good or evil" (Ecclesiastes 12:14).

Here, we see the fascinating and frightening truths about how the unredeemed are judged.

At the Great White Throne, the people whose names are not found written in the Book of Life will stand before God. I believe there will be a searching of that book, because it's God's desire that none would perish (2 Peter 3:9). An angel or some other heavenly creature may be turning the pages, looking for the place where a person's name should be. It can't be found. It's not there. "It's blank," the voice declares. "Your name is not here. Your name is not written in the Lamb's Book of Life." I don't know if it will happen exactly like that, but I believe it could.

> *people whose names are not found written in the Book of Life will stand before God.*

Jesus said, "He who rejects Me, and does not receive My words, has that which judges him – the word that I have spoken will judge him in the last day" (John 12:48). This is a reference to the divine library – the sixty-six books of the Bible that will be opened. Our lives will be judged according to the Word of God. Where we've been obedient and where we've been disobedient will be revealed.

Then another book will be opened, the Book of Life, to see if our names are written there. Some will be missing. There will be blank places. So all those who have died without Christ, all those who have entered eternity without knowing Jesus Christ as Lord and Savior, will be standing at this Great White Throne judgment.

Everyone at that judgment, whose names are not found in the Book of Life, will be cast into the Lake of Fire, where they will be forever.

Is your name written in the Lamb's Book of Life? Are you sure? Perhaps you have heard the Gospel – how Christ died for your sins as the Scriptures say. You know He was buried and rose again on the third day, exactly as predicted. Some people attend church only on Christmas and Easter, but you attend more often than that. You've heard that you should give your life to Christ – "to repent and believe" as the preacher called it. You know you need to trust Him as your Savior, because He's your only hope to get into Heaven. If you were to die tonight, you won't get a second chance to accept His invitation. I encourage you, right now, to get on your knees, repent of your sin, and say yes to Jesus.

What does a sinner say to God? Be as open and honest as you can be, because if you're not, you're not fooling anybody but yourself. He knows your heart, so go ahead and let yourself go. You've made plenty of mistakes in your life, so admit the ones that come to mind and express your desire to receive Jesus into your heart.

Using your own words, you can pray something like this: "Lord Jesus, I know that I am a sinner and I do not deserve eternal life. But, I believe You died and rose from the grave to make me a new creation and to prepare me to dwell in your presence forever. Jesus, come into my life, take control of my life, forgive my sins, and save me. I am now placing my trust in You alone for my salvation, and I accept your free gift of eternal life."

All this time, Jesus has been knocking at the door, asking people if He could come in, but millions remain, still unsaved.

Refusing to repent of their sins, they haven't invited Him in. They will be the ones who have believed a lie, who would be deceived by the Antichrist during the tribulation. Their final fate will be seen at the Great White Throne when they are judged and cast into the Lake of Fire. You need to be sure you're not in that group.

Back in verse 13, we see that Death and Hades will be delivered up, cast into the Lake of Fire. The Greek word *hades* is sometimes translated *hell*, but the intended meaning is the same, referring to the place where people go when they die, not the place of eternal judgment, which is the Lake of Fire. In this "underworld" region, a great divide separates two sides. One is *Paradise*, where the righteous reside in perfect peace. The other is what we typically refer to as *Hell*, a place of torment.

In Luke 16:19–31, we learn a little about the underworld when Jesus tells a story about the death of a rich man. A beggar named Lazarus also died and went to Paradise, where he went to be with Abraham and all the believing saints of the Old Testament. The rich man was on the other side of the great divide, in torment, not because he was rich but because he had refused to repent of his sins.

In 1 Samuel 28:6–15, we learn about Samuel coming back from Paradise and appearing to King Saul. In predicting His own death and resurrection, Jesus referred to Jonah when He said, "For as Jonah was three days and three nights in the belly of the great fish, so will the Son of Man be three days and three nights in the heart of the earth" (Matthew 12:40). The apostle Paul said that when Jesus rose from the dead, He "led captivity captive" (Ephesians 4:8–10), emptying Paradise of its inhabitants and taking them with him to His Father's house (John 14:2–3).

Today, "to be absent from the body is to be present with the Lord" (2 Corinthians 5:8). When those who have accepted Christ die, they go directly to Heaven. Having been caught up in the Spirit, seeing what Heaven was like (2 Corinthians 12:2), the apostle Paul was torn between two desires, one to remain on earth, the other "to depart and be with Christ, which is far better" (Philippians 1:23).

As Christians, we have the assurance that we don't have to go to Paradise, waiting for a day when we can be with Christ. We go to the mansions in Heaven because Jesus sprinkled His blood on the altar there, giving us immediate access to the Father.

Now, the only residents of the underworld *Hades*, in what we call *Hell*, are those who are not with Christ but await judgment at the Great White Throne. We read about the sons of Korah who rebelled against Moses, who were swallowed alive by the earth and were taken directly to "the pit," meaning Hell (Numbers 16:31–33). When the Bible says "Sheol has enlarged herself" (Isaiah 5:14), the prophet is speaking of the day when the Paradise side of the underworld would be taken over as a place of torment.

> *We go to the mansions in Heaven because Jesus sprinkled His blood on the altar there*

The rebellious angels who became demons will be judged as well. We are told that "God did not spare the angels who sinned, but cast them down to hell and delivered them into chains of darkness, to be reserved for judgment" (2 Peter 2:4). The word translated *Hell* in this verse refers to *Tartarus*, the Greek name for the bottomless pit, where some of the fallen angels remain to this day, waiting for their day of judgment. You may recall the time when a legion of demons begged Jesus not to send them to that place but were permitted to enter a herd of pigs instead (Luke 8:30–32).

There are many compartments to this spiritual underworld of punishment. The final and lasting place is the Lake of Fire. As this chapter closes, time, the earth, and evil will end forever.

It is the last day, the day of the Lord.

Chapter 21

Now we come to a much more pleasant subject. We get to tour the city of Heaven.

Cities that are overcrowded, dirty, and crime-prone are struggling to gain a positive image. John reveals a quite different city, a place where everybody should want to live. If Jesus is your Lord and Savior, you already have property there. Jesus said, "In My Father's house are many mansions; if it were not so, I would have told you. I go to prepare a place for you" (John 14:2).

A mansion is already built for you in Heaven, just waiting for the day when you will arrive.

We begin with the descent of the city.

> [1] Now I saw a new heaven and a new earth, for the first heaven and the first earth had passed away. Also there was no more sea. [2] Then I, John, saw the holy city, New Jerusalem, coming down out of heaven from God, prepared as a bride adorned for her husband.

The earth will be purged by fire. "The day of the Lord will come as a thief in the night, in which the heavens will pass away with a great noise, and the elements will melt with fervent heat;

both the earth and the works that are in it will be burned up" (2 Peter 3:10). This is the destruction of the cosmos. The atmosphere of the earth will be purged. Just as Noah's flood purged the earth, so fire will purge the earth in that day. The present earth and atmosphere will not cease to exist, but will be cleansed before the heavenly city descends.

Just as Noah's flood purged the earth, so fire will purge the earth in that day.

We have a number of verses that talk about the dwellers in the city. Who's going to be there? Let's look.

> [3] And I heard a loud voice from heaven saying, "Behold, the tabernacle of God is with men, and He will dwell with them, and they shall be His people. God Himself will be with them and be their God.

So our wonderful, loving God will be there.

> [4] "And God will wipe away every tear from their eyes; there shall be no more death, nor sorrow, nor crying. There shall be no more pain, for the former things have passed away."

During the tribulation, even during the millennium, there will be death and tears, great sorrow, and much crying. But when we enter the eternal age, we will leave time and experience eternity. Then God will wipe away all tears from our eyes.

> [5] Then He who sat on the throne said, "Behold, I make all things new." And He said to me, "Write, for these words are true and faithful."

⁶ And He said to me, "It is done! I am the Alpha and the Omega..."

We know who that person is, don't we? Our redeeming Savior, Jesus.

"...the Beginning and the End. I will give of the fountain of the water of life freely to him who thirsts. ⁷ He who overcomes shall inherit all things, and I will be his God and he shall be My son. ⁸ But the cowardly, unbelieving, abominable, murderers, sexually immoral, sorcerers, idolaters, and all liars shall have their part in the lake which burns with fire and brimstone, which is the second death."

Next we see the bride, the wife of the Lord Jesus. This is the church.

⁹ Then one of the seven angels who had the seven bowls filled with the seven last plagues came to me and talked with me, saying, "Come, I will show you the bride, the Lamb's wife."

¹⁰ And he carried me away in the Spirit to a great and high mountain, and showed me the great city, the holy Jerusalem, descending out of heaven from God, ¹¹ having the glory of God. Her light was like a most precious stone, like a jasper stone, clear as crystal.

¹² Also she had a great and high wall with twelve gates, and twelve angels at the gates, and names written on them, which are the names of the twelve tribes of the children of Israel: ¹³ three gates on the

east, three gates on the north, three gates on the
south, and three gates on the west.

The twelve tribes represent the Father's wife. This is Israel.

[14] Now the wall of the city had twelve foundations,
and on them were the names of the twelve apostles of
the Lamb.

[15] And he who talked with me had a gold reed to
measure the city, its gates, and its wall. [16] The city
is laid out as a square; its length is as great as its
breadth. And he measured the city with the reed:
twelve thousand furlongs. Its length, breadth, and
height are equal. [17] Then he measured its wall: one
hundred and forty-four cubits, according to the measure of a man, that is, of an angel. [18] The construction
of its wall was of jasper; and the city was pure gold,
like clear glass. [19] The foundations of the wall of the
city were adorned with all kinds of precious stones:
the first foundation was jasper, the second sapphire,
the third chalcedony, the fourth emerald, [20] the fifth
sardonyx, the sixth sardius, the seventh chrysolite,
the eighth beryl, the ninth topaz, the tenth chryso-
prase, the eleventh jacinth, and the twelfth amethyst.

[21] The twelve gates were twelve pearls: each individual gate was of one pearl. And the street of the
city was pure gold, like transparent glass. [22] But I
saw no temple in it, for the Lord God Almighty and
the Lamb are its temple. [23] The city had no need of
the sun or of the moon to shine in it, for the glory of
God illuminated it. The Lamb is its light.

So we have our wonderful God, the wife of the Father (Israel), the witness of the church (the bride), and the welcomed peoples who will populate that beautiful city. They will come in and out from the new, refreshed earth.

> ²⁴ And the nations of those who are saved shall walk in its light, and the kings of the earth bring their glory and honor into it.

it's the blood of Jesus that covers us and makes us acceptable in the eyes of the Father.

There will still be kings of the earth. The nations of those who are saved are all the redeemed of all the ages. We'll live there. There will be some on the earth, perhaps in physical bodies, who will bring their glory and honor into it.

> ²⁵ Its gates shall not be shut at all by day (there shall be no night there). ²⁶ And they shall bring the glory and the honor of the nations into it.

> ²⁷ But there shall by no means enter it anything that defiles, or causes an abomination or a lie, but only those who are written in the Lamb's Book of Life.

When we all get to Heaven, what a day that will be! This will give the word *heavenly* a whole new meaning.

If there were evil outside, the gates would have to be closed. But we have already seen the unsaved cast into the Lake of Fire. "The cowardly, unbelieving, abominable, murderers, sexually immoral, sorcerers, idolaters, and all liars shall have their part in the lake which burns with fire and brimstone" (Revelation 21:8).

There will be tears to dry because there will be many who do not make it into the city. So that's the reason He'll have to wipe away all tears. Everyone who has been guilty of at least one sin could be categorically refused entrance into Heaven. But it's the blood of Jesus that covers us and makes us acceptable in the eyes of the Father.

The repeat offenders are those who refused to repent. They are the ones who will never be allowed entrance into the city. They will be cast into the Lake of Fire. Only those whose names are written in the Lamb's Book of Life will be seen in the city of Heaven.

Back in verses 10–23, we read the description of the city. To say the view is "breathtaking" would be a vast understatement. John did his best to find images to represent the magnificent beauty and glory he saw, but when nothing on earth is adequate for comparison, the only way we can appreciate the scene is to be there and see it for ourselves.

> *To fully appreciate the city of Heaven, you'll just have to see it yourself.*

Words cannot capture the panorama of Niagara Falls. Even the documentary films can't duplicate the feeling of actually being there. If you've never been there, my words can't say enough for you to understand what it's like. If you've been to the southern rim of the Grand Canyon to see the depth of color and the awesome splendor of God's creation, then you know that a picture and any amount of words isn't enough to tell the whole story.

To fully appreciate the city of Heaven, you'll just have to see it yourself.

It is true about Heaven. It's indescribable. No words are sufficient. Nevertheless, if we will allow our imaginations to soar, John gives us words that hint at the glories we can eagerly anticipate.

There will be no need for street lights in the city, because the glory of God illuminates everything. Jesus is the light of that city.

If you remember the creation story in the book of Genesis, you may have noticed that there was light first, even before God created the sun, moon, and stars. Some scientists have a problem with the order of creation. The skeptics try to make it an issue. Jesus is the light. He was lighting the universe before planets, suns, and galaxies where hung in space.

Look at the layout of the city. You see the expansiveness. Some have calculated it to be 1,500 miles in every direction.

The most important aspect of the city is that the Lamb is there. The presence of Jesus is what makes it Heaven.

Chapter 22

We now see the angelic conclusion to John's vision.

> ¹ And he showed me a pure river of water of life, clear as crystal, proceeding from the throne of God and of the Lamb. ² In the middle of its street, and on either side of the river, was the tree of life, which bore twelve fruits, each tree yielding its fruit every month. The leaves of the tree were for the healing of the nations. ³ And there shall be no more curse, but the throne of God and of the Lamb shall be in it, and His servants shall serve Him. ⁴ They shall see His face, and His name shall be on their foreheads. ⁵ There shall be no night there: They need no lamp nor light of the sun, for the Lord God gives them light. And they shall reign forever and ever.

The tributary of the throne, the water of life, the river of life is flowing in the city. The tree of life was originally in the garden of Eden. Now it's been moved to Heaven and will be returned to the earth during the eternal period.

The tree of life sustained physical life. After they had sinned, Adam and Eve were prohibited from eating from the tree, because if they ate of it, they would live forever in their sinful condition (Genesis 3:22–23).

Possibly, the tree of life will be there so people who have physical bodies can sustain their lives in a perpetual state.

Again we see no need for the sun, because God's presence is their light source. From the throne of God comes the transmission of light.

> [6] Then he said to me, "These words are faithful and true." And the Lord God of the holy prophets sent His angel to show His servants the things which must shortly take place.

> [7] "Behold, I am coming quickly! Blessed is he who keeps the words of the prophecy of this book."

The reliability of these statements is based on the veracity of God's character. The angel seems to be saying that Jesus is coming soon, and we should be ready. The angel, or messenger, who will sound the trumpet may be announcing that the time is at hand.

When I was a young preacher starting in the ministry, I had a friend who preached from this text, "Behold, I come quickly." He said, "Behold, I come quickly," and hit the pulpit really hard. A few folks woke up. He thought, *Well, this is working. I'm going to do it again.*

He backed up a little. "Behold, I come quickly!" he said, hitting the pulpit even harder. A few more people were now alert, staring at him, listening. So he stepped back and shouted, "Behold, I come quickly!" He struck the pulpit so hard, it fell off the platform to the floor below. He felt his face redden, so embarrassed, not knowing what to say.

In a consoling tone, a lady shouted from the congregation, "It's okay. You said you were coming. You gave us fair warning." Jesus has given us fair warning. He's coming soon!

> ⁸ Now I, John, saw and heard these things. And when I heard and saw, I fell down to worship before the feet of the angel who showed me these things.

> ⁹ Then he said to me, "See that you do not do that. For I am your fellow servant, and of your brethren the prophets, and of those who keep the words of this book. Worship God." ¹⁰ And he said to me, "Do not seal the words of the prophecy of this book, for the time is at hand.

"Do not seal the words" means the prophetic vision has been given for public consumption – for *our* benefit. We're supposed to read the words and gain understanding from this book, the Revelation.

The angel then gives a rebuke. The angel gives a revelation and the angel proclaims a reality.

> ¹¹ "He who is unjust, let him be unjust still; he who is filthy, let him be filthy still; he who is righteous, let him be righteous still; he who is holy, let him be holy still."

In verses 12–21, we see a picture of the awesome Christ. The identity of the speaker in the text turns from the angel to the Lord Jesus, who is making His last recorded statements before He ends the Word of God.

Usually, we think of His last statements as being what we call "The Great Commission" – what Jesus told His disciples just before He ascended into Heaven: "It is not for you to know times or seasons which the Father has put in His own authority. But you shall receive power when the Holy Spirit has come upon you; and you shall be witnesses to Me in Jerusalem, and in all Judea and Samaria, and to the end of the earth" (Act 1:7–8).

But now we know that the last words of Jesus are found in the last chapter of the last book in the Bible.

This is it! These are Jesus' last words.

> [12] "And behold, I am coming quickly, and My reward is with Me, to give to every one according to his work. [13] I am the Alpha and the Omega, the Beginning and the End, the First and the Last."

We are to worship the living Word. Jesus is worthy. Next, we see the witness of the written word.

> [14] Blessed are those who do His commandments, that they may have the right to the tree of life, and may enter through the gates into the city. [15] But outside are dogs and sorcerers and sexually immoral and murderers and idolaters, and whoever loves and practices a lie.

There are those who enter the city, and there are those who are excluded forever from the city.

In verses 16 and 17, we hear the welcoming invitation of the living Word.

> [16] "I, Jesus, have sent My angel to testify to you these things in the churches. I am the Root and the Offspring of David, the Bright and Morning Star."

> [17] And the Spirit and the bride say, "Come!" And let him

who hears say, "Come!" And let him who thirsts come. Whoever desires, let him take the water of life freely.

From Genesis to Revelation, God is publicly inviting people to come to Him. Come to Jesus. Anyone can have eternal life. Then we receive a warning about the written Word.

[18] For I testify to everyone who hears the words of the prophecy of this book: If anyone adds to these things, God will add to him the plagues that are written in this book; [19] and if anyone takes away from the words of the book of this prophecy, God shall take away His part from the Book of Life, from the holy city, and from the things which are written in this book.

This warning goes for all Scripture. All Scripture is holy and pure. Those who alter God's Word will experience loss. We find similar warnings in Proverbs 30:6 and Deuteronomy 12:32.

The last two verses express the desire we all should have – a desire for the living Word. Do you want Him? Do you want Jesus?

[20] He who testifies to these things says, "Surely I am coming quickly."

Amen. Even so, come, Lord Jesus!

This is the last prayer in the Bible. We should be praying daily the words of John, "Come, Lord Jesus!"

[21] The grace of our Lord Jesus Christ be with you all. Amen.

We did it! We have experienced the book of Revelation.

Section IV

End-Time Insights

Matthew's Record of the Last Days

We don't know exactly when Jesus will return. It could be today, next week, or next month. Maybe it will be further into the future. Whenever that day comes, where will you be? What will you be doing? What will happen to you? The Bible says the day will come soon. Since we don't know when, and it could be today, we need to be ready right now, working while we wait.

Matthew Chapter 24 answers many of our questions about the end time. In the first verse, we see the setting.

> ¹ Then Jesus went out and departed from the temple, and His disciples came up to show Him the buildings of the temple. ² And Jesus said to them, "Do you not see all these things? Assuredly, I say to you, not one stone shall be left here upon another, that shall not be thrown down."

The disciples were showing Jesus the grandeur of Herod's temple, admiring the magnificent structures on the temple mount, which were among the greatest architectural marvels of their day. Jesus looked beyond the present picture to say all this would soon be destroyed.

> ³ Now as He sat on the Mount of Olives, the disciples came to Him privately, saying, "Tell us, when will these things be? And what will be the sign of Your coming, and of the end of the age?"

After crossing the Kidron Valley, the disciples went up the hillside with Jesus to the Mount of Olives. They knew He was the Messiah, but they were getting some of their facts mixed up. They were looking for a ruling sovereign, not a suffering Savior. They anticipated a crown, not a cross. They expected to rule and reign with Jesus as their king, so the destruction of the temple could not have made sense to them. They wanted to know when the temple compound would be leveled.

> ⁴ And Jesus answered and said to them: "Take heed that no one deceives you. ⁵ For many will come in My name, saying, 'I am the Christ,' and will deceive many. ⁶ And you will hear of wars and rumors of wars. See that you are not troubled; for all these things must come to pass, but the end is not yet. ⁷ For nation will rise against nation, and kingdom against kingdom. And there will be famines, pestilences, and earthquakes in various places. ⁸ All these are the beginning of sorrows."

Jesus was describing the pretribulation period, also known as the Diaspora, the dispersing of the Jewish nation. We call it the "church age," when Jesus gave authority to the church to be His witness. From Antioch, the church turned itself westward.

We can be thankful for the saving of Cornelius and his household (Acts 10:1–48) and the apostle Paul's missionary journeys to reach the Gentiles. Originally, the church was primarily Jewish, and most of us don't have that ancestry.

Fortunately, God's servants crossed ethnic and racial lines in order to bring the Gospel to us.

About AD 70, a little less than forty years after Jesus ascended into Heaven, the Jews rebelled against the Roman Empire and suffered a devastating defeat.

The Roman General Titus and his armies laid siege on Jerusalem. When they entered the city, they didn't destroy all the houses and break down the city walls, but they completely leveled the temple mount, pushing the stones into the valley. Excavations have uncovered some of those stones.

But there's no need to speculate. The Bible plainly tells us when they began.

After their defeat at a final battle at Masada, the Jews were scattered across the civilized world, and the church age was in full swing.

Teachers have offered various speculations on when the last days either have begun or will begin. But there's no need to speculate. The Bible plainly tells us when they began.

On the day of Pentecost, a few days after Jesus ascended into Heaven, the apostle Peter announced the beginning of the last days, saying, "This is what was spoken by the prophet Joel: 'And it shall come to pass in the last days, says God, That I will pour out of My Spirit on all flesh'" (Acts 2:16–17).

You may have seen the Doomsday Clock, a widely recognized clock face that is clicking down to global catastrophe. The hand may be only a few ticks away from the last moments of the last days. Are we now living in the *very* last days? Perhaps. The last hour? That's possible. Since we know we're living in the last days, and nobody really knows the day and hour, we need to be ready now.

The Jews are experiencing a spiritual hard-heartedness, which the Bible says will happen "to Israel until the fullness of the Gentiles has come in" (Romans 11:25). The *fullness* of the Gentiles is a religious term. The *times* of the Gentiles is a political term.

The fullness of the Gentiles began at the cross and will end at the rapture. This is the period from the day the Jews rejected Jesus at the cross, refusing to accept Him as their Messiah, until the day when He comes in the clouds. This is the period when the Gentiles are the spiritual leaders of the world, making up the majority of the church.

The times of the Gentiles started in 586 BC, when Nebuchadnezzar took the Jewish people into exile in Babylon. That event ended the Jews being a great political ruling. Power from then until Jesus comes to rule and reign on earth belongs to the Gentiles. Israel will never be a world super power like the United States, China, or any other world leader.

Israel has been preserved as a nation and will be returned to the land. On May 17, 1948, the Star of David flag rose over the city of Tel Aviv, and Israel became a nation once again, beginning the fulfillment of the promise that God would bring all His people back to the land (Ezekiel 36:24). They aren't all back yet, but one day they will be. Jesus said this would happen.

The disciples also asked, "What will be the sign of the end of the age?" In verses 9–28, Jesus describes what we call the tribulation, a period between the church age and the millennial reign of Christ.

> [9] "Then they will deliver you up to tribulation and kill you, and you will be hated by all nations for My name's sake. [10] And then many will be offended, will betray one another, and will hate one another. [11] Then many false prophets will rise up and deceive many. [12] And because lawlessness will abound, the love of many will grow cold. [13] But he who endures to the end shall be saved. [14] And this gospel of the

kingdom will be preached in all the world as a witness to all the nations, and then the end will come.

[15] "Therefore when you see the 'abomination of desolation,' spoken of by Daniel the prophet, standing in the holy place" (whoever reads, let him understand), [16] "then let those who are in Judea flee to the mountains. [17] Let him who is on the housetop not go down to take anything out of his house. [18] And let him who is in the field not go back to get his clothes. [19] But woe to those who are pregnant and to those who are nursing babies in those days! [20] And pray that your flight may not be in winter or on the Sabbath. [21] For then there will be great tribulation, such as has not been since the beginning of the world until this time, no, nor ever shall be. [22] And unless those days were shortened, no flesh would be saved; but for the elect's sake those days will be shortened.

[23] "Then if anyone says to you, 'Look, here is the Christ!' or 'There!' do not believe it. [24] For false christs and false prophets will rise and show great signs and wonders to deceive, if possible, even the elect. [25] See, I have told you beforehand. [26] Therefore if they say to you, 'Look, He is in the desert!' do not go out; or 'Look, He is in the inner rooms!' do not believe it. [27] For as the lightning comes from the east and flashes to the west, so also will the coming of the Son of Man be. [28] For wherever the carcass is, there the eagles will be gathered together."

The church age ends at the rapture, the catching away of the believers, the redeemed. Next comes the tribulation, and after that, the Lord comes for His saints in the clouds and returns to earth. The return of Jesus will mark the end of the age as we know it. Jesus describes the tribulation and the signs connected with them.

The apostle Paul said the Greeks, or Gentiles, seek after wisdom (1 Corinthians 1:22). We like wisdom. We like to know.

The Jews sought a sign – proof that would make it impossible not to believe. When Jesus healed the paralytic man, He said, "Which is easier, to say to the paralytic, 'Your sins are forgiven you,' or to say, 'Arise, take up your bed and walk'? But that you may know that the Son of Man has power on earth to forgive sins" – He said to the paralytic, "I say to you, arise, take up your bed, and go to your house" (Mark 2:9–11).

Jesus didn't heal just to alleviate the illness of the man. He didn't heal to prove His power. He healed so He might prove His sonship and His Messiahship. He did it as a sign.

At another time, the Jews sought a sign, and Jesus refused, saying "An evil and adulterous generation seeks after a sign, and no sign will be given to it except the sign of the prophet Jonah. For as Jonah was three days and three nights in the belly of the great fish, so will the Son of Man be three days and three nights in the heart of the earth" (Matthew 12:39–40).

Jesus was saying, "I will give you a sign, all right, the greatest sign anyone has ever seen – the power of the resurrection." Yet, they still didn't believe.

The apostle Paul said the purpose of speaking in an unknown language in the church assembly was to convince unbelieving Jews (1 Corinthians 14:21–22), as had been prophesied (Isaiah 28:11). On the day of Pentecost, when unbelieving pilgrims heard strangers speak the language of their countries (Acts 2:1–41), they were convinced by the sign. Believing, they returned home, spreading the Gospel across the lands around the Mediterranean Sea.

Back in Matthew 24:13, we see where Jesus says, "Those who endure to the end shall be saved." He is talking about the physical endurance it takes to make it to the end of the tribulation period, a harrowing time when a third of the people will die. Cataclysmic events will occur, both in nature and at the hand of man. We find the Bible telling us there is a refuge, a hiding place, for the Jewish people. Some Bible students believe it is going to be the city of Petra.

They don't get a "Plan B" alternative to knowing Christ

When President Obama visited the Middle East, he went to Jordan and the city of Petra in the south, which is literally carved out of a mountainside of red stone. People lived there for centuries, but it's now a major tourist attraction, essentially uninhabited.

In verse 14, we learn that the Gospel will be preached to every nation. Some have been misguided into thinking Jesus would come back to preach to everyone.

My book *Embracing the Ends of the Earth* describes the important work we have to do. People around the world need to hear the Gospel. Those who don't know Jesus Christ as their personal Lord and Savior will go to Hell. They don't get a "Plan B" alternative to knowing Christ, who is the only true light "to every man coming into the world" (John 1:9).

If people move toward the light, God will give them more light. But if they turn away, they leave themselves in darkness. Every person in this world has the witness of God's creation, as David's song says, "The heavens declare the glory of God; and the firmament shows His handiwork" (Psalm 19:1).

The law of God is written on the conscience of every heart (Romans 2:15). Inherently, people know what's right and wrong, so we are without excuse (Romans 1:20). A person has to be miseducated into atheism, miseducated into communism, miseducated into humanism.

We are all born with an opportunity to recognize our Creator and are given a nature and need to worship Him. God is witnessing to everyone through creation. He can speak of His existence through the beauty of the landscape, a baby in your arms, or the wonders of outer space. Everywhere in His creation, He is saying, "I am here."

Our conscience and creation are not enough to satisfy people's natural need to worship. They have to hear about the cross. Only Jesus can cleanse their sins. Only the cross can make them right in the eyes of a holy God.

Some people have the idea that as soon as we take the Gospel of the kingdom around the world as a witness to all nations, Matthew 24:14 will be fulfilled and Jesus will have to return. The problem with that theory is that this verse is talking about the tribulation, not the church age. It's talking about an angel who will preach the Gospel during the tribulation (Revelation 14:6).

In the church age, it's our job to preach the Gospel. I'm talking about what we do and say to spread the good news, not just what is spoken from the pulpit at church. At work and play, the people we associate with need to hear the Gospel.

Verse 15 describes the aggression that will take place in the temple. This obviously can't refer to a past or present temple, because no temple is there. This is the temple that will exist during the tribulation, called the "abomination of desolation" midway through the period (Daniel 9:27). The Antichrist will break the treaty by setting up an image of himself, creating an abomination in the temple.

Jesus has answered the disciples' question about the end of the age, the "time of Jacob's trouble" (Jeremiah 30:7). The Jewish people will be once again dealt with in a very special and direct way by the Lord. This is not the same as the end of the world.

Next, Jesus answers the disciples' question, "What will be the sign of your coming?"

> [29] "Immediately after the tribulation of those days the sun will be darkened, and the moon will not give its light; the stars will fall from heaven, and the powers of the heavens will be shaken. [30] Then the sign of the Son of Man will appear in heaven, and then all the tribes of the earth will mourn, and they will see the Son of Man coming on the clouds of heaven with power and great glory. [31] And He will send His angels with a great sound of a trumpet, and they will gather together His elect from the four winds, from one end of heaven to the other."

After the tribulation, the sun will be darkened, the moon won't shine, and the stars will fall. The powers of the heavens will be shaken. People wanted a sign. Now they get one in which all the tribes of the earth will mourn – the Son of Man coming on the clouds of heaven with power and great glory. At the trumpet sound, His angels will gather His elect.

Right now, we're living in the church age. Next comes the tribulation. As Jesus lays out the timeline, His millennial reign follows the tribulation. The only sign people will have at that time is His coming back to this earth – His literal, physical return.

Every eye shall behold Him, even of those who pierced Him (Revelation 1:7). Jesus will come in the clouds. The Jewish people will see Him. Those who haven't received Him as Messiah will receive Him as Messiah.

In that day, God says, "I will seek to destroy all the nations that come against Jerusalem. And I will pour on the house of David and on the inhabitants of Jerusalem the Spirit of grace and supplication; then they will look on Me whom they pierced. Yes, they will mourn for Him as one mourns for his only son, and grieve for Him as one grieves for a firstborn. In that day there shall be a great mourning in Jerusalem, like the mourning at Hadad Rimmon in the plain of Megiddo" (Zechariah 12:9–11).

Armageddon is at Megiddo, located in the north central part of Israel. The battle could stretch from that point to Jerusalem.

the Mount of Olives shall be split in two, from east to west

Israel will recognize its Messiah. In one day, the nation will be born (Isaiah 56:8). This isn't talking about the physical sovereignty of a nation, as we saw on May 17, 1948. No, this is talking about the spiritual birth of a nation, when the Jews will believe on their Messiah. Those who are left will come to know Him.

In that day, Jesus' feet "will stand on the Mount of Olives, which faces Jerusalem on the east. And the Mount of Olives shall be split in two, from east to west, making a very large valley; half of the mountain shall move toward the north and half of it toward the south" (Zechariah 14:4). This prophecy is not figurative, not a metaphor, but an actual geological event when Jesus puts His foot on the Mount of Olives. The place where Jesus ascended will be the place where He returns (Acts 1:11–12).

> "Then you shall flee through My mountain valley, for the mountain valley shall reach to Azal. Yes, you shall flee as you fled from the earthquake in the days of Uzziah king of Judah. Thus the LORD my God will come, and all the saints with You" (Zechariah 14:5).
>
> "And the LORD shall be King over all the earth. In that day it shall be – 'The LORD is one,' and His name one" (Zechariah 14:9).
>
> "And it shall come to pass that everyone who is left

of all the nations which came against Jerusalem shall go up from year to year to worship the King, the LORD of hosts, and to keep the Feast of Tabernacles" (Zechariah 14:16).

The millennial reign of Christ will be a glorious time. Old Testament prophecies sometimes had dualistic meanings. This is a fulfillment of the One who is to come. In those verses, we can plainly see that if the king is the Lord of Hosts, we're talking about a time when Jesus will sit upon the throne of David in the city of Jerusalem. This is a literal fulfillment of the prophecies.

The disciples said, "Jesus, tell us." They were eager to hear. Do you know the problem we have? We want to know more and more and more. I think that's great. We ought to learn as much as we can about God's work. But we are not to be hearers only. We must be doers, applying what we know.

If we really believe this prophecy, we must be burdened for those who do not know Jesus as their Lord and Savior. We must share the Gospel with them. We must live a holy life before them. We must be committed to Jesus' bride, the church.

> [32] "Now learn this parable from the fig tree: When its branch has already become tender and puts forth leaves, you know that summer is near. [33] So you also, when you see all these things, know that it is near – at the doors! [34] Assuredly, I say to you, this generation will by no means pass away till all these things take place. [35] Heaven and earth will pass away, but My words will by no means pass away. [36] But of that day and hour no one knows, not even the angels of heaven, but My Father only.

> [37] "But as the days of Noah were, so also will the

coming of the Son of Man be. [38] For as in the days before the flood, they were eating and drinking, marrying and giving in marriage, until the day that Noah entered the ark, [39] and did not know until the flood came and took them all away, so also will the coming of the Son of Man be.

[40] "Then two men will be in the field: one will be taken and the other left. [41] Two women will be grinding at the mill: one will be taken and the other left. [42] Watch therefore, for you do not know what hour your Lord is coming.

[43] "But know this, that if the master of the house had known what hour the thief would come, he would have watched and not allowed his house to be broken into. [44] Therefore you also be ready, for the Son of Man is coming at an hour you do not expect."

Our knowledge of truth is a call to action. We know Jesus is coming, and the time is short.

We have said, "Tell us, Jesus," and He has told us: "Be ready. You don't know the day or the hour." It could be right now.

Christ's Triumphant Return

Every year on Easter Sunday, we hear a message about Jesus' resurrection. Whenever we celebrate the Lord's Supper, we are reminded of Jesus' words: "Do this in remembrance of me" (Luke 22:19). We remember what Christ has done for us, how He was crucified, was buried, and on the third day rose again. Once we were condemned to death, and now we appreciate the fact that He has brought us life. If that's true, then we should also anticipate His promise, as yet unfulfilled.

The apostle Paul said, "For as often as you eat this bread and drink this cup, you proclaim the Lord's death till He comes" (1 Corinthians 11:26). What are we anticipating when we remember His resurrection? We're thinking about when He will return, looking forward to the day when we will see Him face-to-face.

In Acts Chapter 1, we learn that Jesus was on earth forty days after the resurrection, appearing to people, proving that He was, in fact, the resurrected Lord. Just before He was to ascend into Heaven, His disciples asked, "Lord, will You at this time restore the kingdom to Israel?" (Acts 1:6). After following Jesus and working with Him in ministry for three years, after being with Him at different times for almost six weeks following the resurrection, this is the one question they felt was most important before He left. You see, they were still looking for a political, military deliverer.

After teaching His disciples for three years, this is the answer Jesus knew they most needed to hear before He ascended to Heaven. In today's language, He might have said, "I am coming back, but you don't get to know when. In the meantime, you have a lot of work to do." Then He was lifted into the air and disappeared behind the clouds. As the disciples were still looking up, two men, dressed in white, appeared beside them and said, "Men of Galilee, why do you stand gazing up into heaven? This same Jesus, who was taken up from you into heaven, will so come in like manner as you saw Him go into heaven" (Acts 1:11).

What an interesting situation. Of all the questions the disciples might have asked after three years, this one stands out as most important: "Lord, will You at this time restore the kingdom to Israel?"

Many Old Testament passages speak of the Messiah who will come as the King, One who will come as ruler over Israel, One who will reestablish the nation as the political center of the world. Today, only a few million Jews inhabit a sliver of land along the eastern Mediterranean, just seventeen miles across at its narrowest point and a couple hundred miles long.

Right now, Israel is not the world's greatest political or military power. Other nations are more powerful, such as China, Russia, the United States, European nations, even North Korea. The Arab nations surrounding Israel are forces that hold great sway. After two thousand years, Israel remains only a small force among many powerful forces, far from being dominant.

The disciples were looking for the day when their Messiah would soon return and reestablish Israel as the dominant nation on earth. I believe the Bible teaches that this will happen one day. Perhaps, one day soon.

Israel may not be the dominant political and military power today, but it is a major focal point of concern for people and nations around the world.

In response to the disciples' question, Jesus said, "It is not for you to know times or seasons which the Father has put in His own authority. But you shall receive power when the Holy Spirit has come upon you; and you shall be witnesses to Me in Jerusalem, and in all Judea and Samaria, and to the end of the earth" (Acts 1:7–8).

But just like those disciples, we still want to speculate about the future.

The book of Revelation would come many years later. Right now, the disciples were not to allow their concern for the future stand in the way of doing what was needed in the present – witnessing for Christ, testifying of His resurrection power, preaching the kingdom of God, making disciples.

Jesus was giving marching orders to the church – to go everywhere and tell others about Him. But just like those disciples, we still want to speculate about the future. Why? Perhaps we want to be prepared. We feel like we need to know how much time we have left. Whatever that time is, it isn't enough. The time is short, so we need to be busy spreading the good news.

We look at the events in the Middle East and see constant turmoil. Political and religious persecution is escalating with tens of thousands of innocent people being injured or killed. Then we wonder, *Is this the beginning of the very last moments of the last time?*

People have an insatiable appetite for knowing more about the future. They consult our horoscopes. Palm readers, psychics, cultists, and occultists, prey on people who want to know what lies ahead. What does the future hold? How bad will it be? Will it get better? How will we survive? The questions are endless, because desperate people need security and don't know how to find it in the Lord.

Current events give us little reason to be optimistic. The American church is on the decline. Our culture seems to be losing its moral stability. Public riots, school shootings, and acts of terrorism have become so common that we're no longer surprised when we hear the news. Some of us wonder, *Is there any hope for our nation?*

As bad as conditions are right now, they can still get worse.

But there is good news. Those who live and believe in Christ don't have to worry about dying. As Jesus told Martha only a few days before He was arrested, tried, and crucified, "I am the resurrection and the life. He who believes in Me, though he may die, he shall live" (John 11:25). The Lord knows those who belong to Him (2 Timothy 2:19), and we will be safe, regardless.

There is more good news for those who follow our Lord Jesus Christ. One day soon, He is coming again. Are you ready? That day is as certain as recorded history. As sure as when Jesus was born in Bethlehem, lived a sinless life, died at Calvary, and rose from the dead, He is coming again, and when He does, we are to be ready.

What the angels said to the disciples is important if we are to know what to expect. In Acts 1:9, Luke repeatedly uses the personal pronouns "He" and "Him" referring to the Son of Man, Jesus, who had been the disciples' Teacher and Master for three years. Then the angels say in verse 11, "This same Jesus will so come in like manner as you saw Him go." So the next big event on Jesus' itinerary is His return to earth. We will see the same person who ascended into the clouds descend from the clouds.

Some who look for clues about the last days spend a lot of energy looking for signs – something to indicate how close we are to the coming of Christ. They will compare the number of recent earthquakes with a thousand years ago and say, "We have many more now. The end must be near." While that may be true, the numbers aren't reliable evidence of anything, since we didn't have super-sensitive, seismic monitors a thousand years ago. Some will speculate about who the Antichrist is, taking the number 666 and matching it with the numerical value of the letters in a person's name. Such practices have been going on for centuries, but to no avail.

If we're tempted to get carried away into looking for signs and ways to calculate when the end will be, we need to understand that being ready is not about figuring out signs. It's about knowing our Savior. We're looking for a person. The very next item on God's timetable of big events is the return of Jesus Christ.

Some people deny that there will ever be a literal return. "When Jesus comes into our hearts," they say, "that's the second coming." That view ignores what the angels told the disciples – that Jesus would be returning in the same manner in which He left. Certainly, we need Christ in our hearts, but there will be a day when Jesus will descend from the clouds. We are to anticipate that time and be ready.

One cult has said that Jesus arrived secretly in 1914 and set up His millennial kingdom. Someone may have knocked on your door, talked to you about their doctrine, and wanted you to buy some of their books. Their message can't be true, which we learned in our study of the book of Revelation. We know that during the millennium, the Devil will be locked away in chains (Revelation 20:2), and that definitely isn't the condition we see on earth today. Since we're far from living in a time of peace and brotherly love, it's absurd to believe Jesus secretly came and established His kingdom a hundred years ago.

Another belief says the last days began in 1844, when Jesus supposedly entered the Holy of Holies, but that can't be right. From the Bible, we know exactly when the last days began – on the day of Pentecost that followed the day when Jesus ascended into Heaven. On that day when the Holy Spirit was poured out, Peter stood before the people and said, "This is what was spoken by the prophet Joel: and it shall come to pass in the last days, says God, that I will pour out of My Spirit on all flesh" (Acts 2:16-17). From that moment until now, the last days have been marching

When Jesus comes, we will definitely recognize Him

forward. After almost two thousand years, we might say we're in the last seconds of the last minute of the last hour of the last day of the last days. Compared to where we were back then, Jesus must be coming very soon.

When Jesus comes, we will definitely recognize Him, because He is the crucified Christ. Hundreds of years before Jesus was born, Old Testament prophets foretold Jesus coming to die for our sins: "I will pour on the house of David and on the inhabitants of Jerusalem the Spirit of grace and supplication; then they will look on Me whom they pierced" (Zechariah 12:10). Consistent with what the angels said would happen after Jesus ascended, John writes: "Behold, He is coming with clouds, and every eye will see Him, even they who pierced Him" (Revelation 1:7).

You see, God is holy, perfect, and sinless. Without exception, we're all sinners. None of us can measure up to God's standard. Therefore, we fall short of the glory of God (Romans 3:23). None of us are perfect. Because of our sinfulness, our lack of ability to keep all of God's commandments, we fall short and unavoidably come under the judgment of a holy God. If it weren't for what Christ accomplished on the cross, I would get what I deserved – death. Apart from Christ, the consequence of sin is death (Romans 6:23), making it impossible for me to enter Heaven.

I love my wife and children. I read the Bible and try to live a good life. And yet, if I got what I deserved, there would be no place for me in Heaven. I would be separated from God, destined for Hell. All my righteous deeds wouldn't be enough to save me from the Lake of Fire, because without Christ, I'm still a sinner.

Listen! Jesus came to die on the cross, with His own blood taking the punishment for our sins. "God demonstrates His own love toward us, in that while we were still sinners, Christ died for us" (Romans 5:8). His sacrifice, if we will accept Him, means we're justified – made as if we had never sinned. When our sins have been covered by His blood, we know we're going to Heaven. If Jesus were to return this very moment, we would go to meet Him in the air.

To be made righteous in God's eyes, what must we do?

First, we must repent, a biblical term that means we turn away from our sinful desires and accept Jesus as our Savior, making Him Lord, choosing to follow him. That's what repentance is all about – giving our lives to Him, so what He wants is more important than what we want, as Jesus prayed before He was arrested: "Not My will, but Yours, be done" (Luke 22:42).

Believing is the next step, a step of faith, to trust, rely upon, and accept what He has said He would do for us upon the cross: to forgive us of our sins. He is the living Lord, and we are to receive Him as Lord. He is our Savior, the One we are to trust for the forgiveness of sin.

If you have never received Jesus into your heart as your personal Lord and Savior, there is no better time than right now. Tomorrow might be too late, so don't put off what you most need today.

When you ask Him into your heart, you don't have to use fancy words. Just be open and honest, because He already knows. You can pray something like this: "Lord Jesus, I know that I am a sinner, and I do not deserve eternal life. But, I believe You died and rose from the grave to make me a new creation and to prepare me to dwell in your presence forever. Jesus, come into my life, take control of my life, forgive my sins and save me. I am now placing my trust in You alone for my salvation, and I accept your free gift of eternal life."

Saved by His grace, you are ready for whenever the Lord comes.

His arrival is in two phases. First, He will come in the clouds *for* His saints, taking us to Heaven. Seven years later, He will come back to earth *with* His saints. Then He will fulfill what the disciples were expecting before Jesus ascended into the clouds. He will be the conquering commander, when "the armies in Heaven, clothed in fine linen, white and clean, followed Him on white horses" (Revelation 19:14).

Jesus holds the sword and will bring judgment upon the earth, setting inequities right, making the crooked path straight. He is the conquering commander, the coming king, who will rule and reign for a thousand years. He will sit upon the throne of David, and Israel will be the center of political and religious power.

Philosophers don't have the answers. Secular humanists cannot alleviate our pain and suffering. The skeptic gives us no hope. Scientists cannot raise the dead. Only Jesus can meet all our needs. He alone is our answer.

Looking for signs is a waste of time. Look for the person – Jesus. He could come at any time. Not one prophecy has to be fulfilled. The temple in Jerusalem doesn't have to be rebuilt. There are no other signs we are to look for. We are to look for a person – the Lord Jesus Christ.

Remember the angels' promise after Jesus ascended into Heaven. "Why do you stand gazing up into heaven? This same Jesus, who was taken up from you into heaven, will so come in like manner as you saw Him go into heaven" (Acts 1:11).

The Old Testament is pregnant with messianic promises, saying even more about the second coming than it does the first. All Scripture, both the Old Testament and the New, speaks of His coming. I believe the next big event on God's calendar is Jesus coming in the clouds to catch away the redeemed. We call it the rapture, the ascension of those who know Christ, to be with Him in Heaven. This could happen at any moment.

> "For the Lord Himself will descend from heaven with a shout, with the voice of an archangel, and with the trumpet of God. And the dead in Christ will rise first. Then we who are alive and remain shall be caught up together with them in the clouds to meet the Lord in the air. And thus we shall always be with the Lord" (1 Thessalonians 4:16–17).

Isn't that wonderful? Jesus is coming.

If you have lost loved ones – parents, children, siblings, or friends who have gone to be with the Lord – when Jesus comes in the clouds, there will be a great wake-up call when the bodies of the righteous dead will be raised.

We may not understand how God will bring together the molecular structure of those who have died long ago, but we can be sure the Creator of life is fully capable. We read on the first page of our Bibles, "In the beginning, God…" and it was so. The same God who stepped out on nothing – who spoke into nothing and caused the worlds to exist – He who brought life in the beginning will raise the righteous from their graves to live forever with Him.

The Bible says, "Beloved, now we are children of God; and it has not yet been revealed what we shall be, but we know that when He is revealed, we shall be like Him, for we shall see Him as He is" (1 John 3:2). We don't know exactly what our resurrected bodies will be like, but we know we will be like Jesus after He was raised from the dead.

What an amazing event is about to happen, in a moment, in the blink of an eye (1 Corinthians 15:52). In a split second, we will be transformed, translated, and made like Jesus, caught up to be with Him in the air. What a tremendous moment that will be. Do you know when it could happen? Right now. Hopefully, we'll be caught doing something good for Him, not something we shouldn't be doing.

Jesus said, "Let not your heart be troubled; you believe in God, believe also in Me. In My Father's house are many mansions; if it were not so, I would have told you. I go to prepare a place for you. And if I go and prepare a place for you, I will come again and receive you to Myself; that where I am, there you may be also" (John 14:1–3). Where is Jesus right now? In Heaven, and He's coming to receive us to Himself.

His return will be in the clouds to catch us away to be with Him, and we're looking for that return. He's also coming for the same people who love Him and who know Him. His arrival will be like a thief who slips in at night without warning, when it's too late for those who are sleeping, who aren't ready, who aren't watching (Revelation 16:15).

If a thief broke into your house, he wouldn't be there to take out your garbage. No, he would be looking for furs, jewelry, guns – items of great earthly value.

When Jesus comes, He will take what is most precious to Him – those who have been bought and paid for by His blood. He's coming for us.

In the second phase of His second coming, when He returns to earth *with* His saints, He's coming to the same place. He ascended from the Mount of Olives, and He will come back to the same place. "And in that day His feet will stand on the Mount of Olives, which faces Jerusalem on the east. And the Mount of Olives shall be split in two, from east to west, making a very large valley; half of the mountain shall move toward the north and half of it toward the south" (Zechariah 14:4).

If you've ever visited the Mount of Olives, you know that it hasn't yet split. That day will come at the end of the seven tribulation years, when He comes back as the conquering commander and as the coming king to set up His kingdom. He'll put His foot right there on top of the Mount of Olives, in the same place from where He ascended.

The Bible will be proven credible to an incredulous world. Jesus has invaded history and now infuses reality and inhabits eternity. He is Lord of the universe. When He returns, there will be no question who He is. Listen to the promise. He is coming again.

they're telling us to live with a purpose.

In World War II, General MacArthur made a promise to the Filipino people, saying, "I shall return." Cameras were flashing when he waded ashore, recapturing the islands of the Philippines. He had kept his promise. We can be sure, when Jesus has said, "I will return," He will keep His promise.

After Jesus ascended into Heaven, the angel said to the disciples, "Men of Galilee, why do you stand gazing up into heaven?" (Acts 1:11). In these words, the angel is telling the disciples to live with a purpose, and they're telling us to live with a purpose.

I must admit, if I had been watching Jesus ascend into Heaven, I too would be standing there in amazement, gazing at the clouds, hoping for one last glimpse of His departure.

The angel was saying, "Live with a purpose. It's time to quit standing there. You need to get moving to fulfill God's purpose for your life."

Rick Warren became well known because of his bestselling book *The Purpose Driven Life*. His message was translated into many languages and swept across the world because people want meaning for their lives. They wanted to understand their purpose, but they didn't know what to do. Sadly, without a feeling of purpose, when they fail to recognize that their lives have value, some people commit suicide.

Jesus is coming, and recognition of that fact gives us insight about where we are headed and what we need to be doing right now. It's not about this life only, as the apostle Paul said: "If in this life only we have hope in Christ, we are of all men the most pitiable" (1 Corinthians 15:19). Life is also about what lies ahead for us – what some people call the "sweet by and by."

The great preacher Jerry Vines once said, "When we believe He will take us up, it will clean us up and cheer us up." The Bible says that the hope of His return will purify us (1 John 3:3). If we're expecting Jesus to come at any moment, we will naturally be living a more holy life, directing our actions to what most pleases Him.

The loss of a loved one may bring sadness and hardship, but there is a comfort that will help us rise from our grief. The apostle Paul said, "I do not want you to be ignorant, brethren, concerning those who have fallen asleep, lest you sorrow as others who have no hope. For if we believe that Jesus died and rose again, even so God will bring with Him those who sleep in Jesus" (1 Thessalonians 4:13–14). We can comfort one another with the knowledge that we will be "caught up together with them in the clouds to meet the Lord in the air. And thus we shall always be with the Lord" (1 Thessalonians 4:17).

While we look "for the blessed hope and glorious appearing of our great God and Savior Jesus Christ," we become "zealous for good works" (Titus 2:13–14). Since we don't know when He's coming, we watch for Him (Matthew 25:13), and we work for Him.

One day, "we must all appear before the judgment seat of Christ." There will be two great judgments, one for the

Christian, the other for the unbeliever. Each person will be judged "according to what he has done, whether good or bad" (2 Corinthians 5:10).

The Bible says, "No other foundation can anyone lay than that which is laid, which is Jesus Christ. Now if anyone builds on this foundation with gold, silver, precious stones, wood, hay, straw, each one's work will become clear; for the Day will declare it, because it will be revealed by fire; and the fire will test each one's work, of what sort it is" (1 Corinthians 3:11–13).

Those who have not accepted Christ will face the second judgment, a terrible judgment of unbelievers called the Great White Throne Judgment (Revelation 20:11–15). People need to give their hearts to Jesus right now, because they don't get a second chance after death.

We face one of two unavoidable realities: either we die or we live to see the return of Jesus. Personally, I'm looking for the upper-taker, not the undertaker, the cloud route, not the clod route. But when we know Jesus as our Savior, either way takes us into His presence.

One day when we stand before Him, we can hear Him say, "Well done, good and faithful servant."

So my desire is to stand before Him one day and hear Him say, "Well done, good and faithful servant."

As songwriter Elizabeth Mills wrote:

Oh land of rest, for thee I sigh! When will the moment come when I shall lay my armor by and dwell in peace at home? We'll work till Jesus comes, We'll work 'till Jesus comes, We'll work till Jesus comes, And we will be gathered home. To Jesus Christ I fled for rest; He bade me cease to roam and lean for comfort on His breast till He conduct me home. We'll work till Jesus comes, We'll work till Jesus comes, We'll work till Jesus comes, And we'll be gathered home.

We will live each day expecting His return. Living with a purpose. Looking for a person. Listening to the promise.

The Rapture and the Golden Age

The next big event on God's timetable is the rapture, which is the coming of the Lord in the air. When Jesus arrives, we'll be transported to Heaven, where we will be with Him during the seven years of tribulation on earth. After that, Jesus will return with us to earth, literally and bodily for a one-thousand-year reign.

Time ends. Eternity begins. We're with Him forever and ever.

If you haven't already, now is the time to make your reservation for the heavenly city.

Jesus could come today. Like the little boy said when he saw his Boxer puppy's cropped tail, "It won't be long now," we see the time is short. Jesus is coming soon. Let's be ready for the Golden Age when Jesus rules on earth for a thousand years.

Are you an optimist or a pessimist? Is the glass half full or half empty? If we pay attention to what is going on in this country, if we recognize the moral decay in our culture, if some churches seem more like country clubs than worship centers, we have reason to grieve and be concerned about our future. The glass seems half empty and steadily going down. Will conditions ever get better? Yes. We can be positive, knowing these problems will end soon. Everything will be better when Jesus comes, when we're caught up to be with Him.

For a thousand years on earth, Jesus will be universally recognized as Lord.

Theologians have three main views about this period, which we call the "millennium."

Amillenialism has been a popular view through the years, which simply means "there is no millennium." In the end time, there will be one great judgment after Jesus comes in the clouds to take us away. They don't believe He will come to earth. Jesus will simply end time, and eternity begins.

Some in this group don't believe in salvation by grace. They interpret the judgment of the nations in Matthew 25 as a judgment based on the works of every individual. The sheep represent those who are saved and go to Heaven. The goats represent those who are lost and go to Hell.

Amillennialists who believe in salvation by grace, including some Baptists, believe we'll just go to be with Jesus in Heaven. They don't believe Jesus will come to rule and reign with us on earth.

Postmillennialism believes in a worldwide revival that will bring such widespread salvation and change of hearts that Jesus will come back. The thousand years of peace that follows will be a result of this great evangelistic effort. This view was common in the late 1800s but lost its appeal during World War I and virtually disappeared. Variations of this belief do seem to be making a comeback in some areas.

Premillennialism believes Jesus will reign on earth for a thousand years.

Numerous views exist about the tribulation period. Some share my belief that the saints will be caught away to be with Jesus in Heaven and not have to suffer through the tribulation on earth. Others believe the saints will be raptured in the middle of the tribulation, before conditions get really bad. Those who believe in a posttribulation rapture say everyone will be caught away the end of the tribulation to await a final judgment.

I can't speak for everyone else, but I don't want to go through the tribulation. I believe the Bible teaches that we'll be caught away *before* the tribulation begins. I am what we might call a "pretribulation rapturist" and "dispensational premillennialist."

> *I don't know exactly how all that will work, but we know enough from the Bible to be excited.*

All the views I have described fit within the Baptist Faith and Message statement of the Southern Baptist Convention. You can be pre-, post-, or a-millennial. You can be pre-, mid-, or post-tribulation. The statement of faith doesn't make that choice about the end times. Any of these positions still fit within the family of Southern Baptists.

We should always be seeking to know the biblical truth. I'm looking for Jesus Christ, not the Antichrist. I'm looking for the rapture, not tribulation. I'm listening for the trumpet sound when Jesus will arrive in the clouds and catch me away to be with Him in Heaven.

When Jesus returns to Earth, we who are redeemed will be with Him. In our glorified bodies, we will rule and reign with Him, with responsibilities to oversee. I don't know exactly how all that will work, but we know enough from the Bible to be excited. We will live on a purified earth that has been returned to its glory.

The most important aspect of the Golden Age is that Jesus is King on earth. The literal, physical, visible return of Jesus Christ initiates the transformation of our world. Ruthless dictators, cruel rulers, and deceptive political leaders will no longer govern our society. God-opposing, anti-Christian movements, and various "isms" of false belief that have tried to capture people's hearts will be gone.

When Jesus comes back, He will come as King. Satan will be bound during the millennium.

The angel Gabriel gave a two-part promise about Jesus. "And behold, you will conceive in your womb and bring forth a Son, and shall call His name JESUS. He will be great, and will be called the Son of the Highest; and the Lord God will give Him the throne of His father David. And He will reign over the house of Jacob forever, and of His kingdom there will be no end" (Luke 1:31–33, emphasis added). Mary conceived, brought forth a son, and called Him Jesus. That part has been fulfilled. But Jesus is not yet sitting upon David's throne, reigning forever.

After Jesus ascended into Heaven, we have a promise from another angel. "Men of Galilee, why do you stand gazing up into heaven? This same Jesus, who was taken up from you into heaven, will so come in like manner as you saw Him go into heaven" (Acts 1:11). Jesus literally and bodily ascended from the Mount of Olives, and He will literally and bodily return to the same place.

An angel came to John on the Isle of Patmos to reveal "things which must shortly take place" (Revelation 1:1). Again we see the promise of Jesus coming to rule and reign. "Behold, He is coming with clouds, and every eye will see Him, even they who pierced Him. And all the tribes of the earth will mourn because of Him. Even so, Amen" (Revelation 1:7). When Jesus ascended into Heaven, He hadn't yet been seen by the Jewish people as their Messiah. The majority of the Jewish people are still in unbelief. In the Golden Age, Jesus will come back to the throne of David, to the city of Jerusalem, to rule over the world.

The Jews were given a promise of a coming King. "Behold, the days are coming," says the LORD, "that I will raise to David a Branch of righteousness; a King shall reign and prosper, and execute judgment and righteousness in the earth. In His days Judah will be saved, and Israel will dwell safely; now this is His name by which He will be called: THE LORD OUR RIGHTEOUSNESS" (Jeremiah 23:5–6). No king of Judah or Israel ever bore the title "The Lord Our Righteousness." Since only Jesus has that title, we know for certain that Jesus is coming to be King on earth to rule from Jerusalem (Isaiah 24:23).

The Bible declares that Jerusalem is the throne of the Lord (Jeremiah 3:17). Now that's not some euphemistic sense of a spiritual existence. It is the realty that Jerusalem will be the place where Jesus will reign. Israel will be a strong nation ruled by the Supreme Sovereign (Micah 4:1–13). When Jesus comes back to earth, He will fulfill the promise according to Scripture. He will rule and reign with a rod of iron.

European monarchy today has very little governing power. Much of the glamor connected with the British monarchy derives from history and a continuing fantasy over what it would be like to be ruled by a great king or queen. We love fairytale weddings. Many people bounced out of bed at four o'clock in the morning to watch Princess Diana's marriage to Prince Charles.

We're still looking for the Lord Our Righteousness, the one who will rule in righteousness. "When the righteous are in authority, the people rejoice; but when a wicked man rules, the people groan" (Proverbs 29:2). If there has ever been a time when we needed righteous rulers, it's today. We have none. We see none. We know of none. Yet a righteous ruler will soon come. His name is Jesus. He will be King on earth.

This thousand-year reign has another important aspect: the Jews will once again be the spiritual leaders of the world. After AD 70 when Titus and his army rode into Jerusalem and wiped the temple mount clean, fulfilling Jesus prophecy in Matthew 24:2, few people believed a Jewish nation would ever exist again. Scattered around the world, Jewish people retained their racial ethnicity, and on May 17, 1948, the new nation of Israel was born. They retained their language. They retained their religion. In all those aspects, the Jewish people have been the most hated and despised race on earth for 2000 years. They are in the land of Israel today with their own national identity, but they're there in unbelief.

When Pilate brought Jesus before the people, they cried for His crucifixion, saying, "His blood be on us and on our children" (Matthew 27:25), and it has been, not in the redeeming sense, but in judgment. Yet God's promise to Abraham said, "I give to you and your descendants after you the land in which you are a stranger, all the land of Canaan, as an everlasting possession; and I will be their God" (Genesis 17:8). Not only did God promise the land to Abraham and his descendants, He said He would be their God.

Jerusalem will be the center of all commerce, politics, and worship.

Scripture designates the land to stretch from the Nile River to the Euphrates River, up to modern-day Turkey, and down to the Sinai Peninsula. It will be that entire land mass. Since 1948, world leaders have tried to get the Israeli government to give away land for the sake of peace. Starting with the Camp David Accords during the Carter administration, that's been the mantra of the US government to Israel: "You need to give land for peace. Create a Palestinian state." Yet we can be sure God's Word is true. One day, all the land promised by God will be possessed by the Jewish people.

When Jesus returns, the fullness of the Gentiles will be complete, and religious rule will shift back to Israel. Jerusalem will be the center of all commerce, politics, and worship. God has said to the Jews, "Surely I will take the children of Israel from among the nations, wherever they have gone, and will gather them from every side and bring them into their own land; and I will make them one nation in the land, on the mountains of Israel; and one king shall be king over them all" (Ezekiel

37:21–22). One king is promised, not a prime minister and parliament as Israel has now. Jesus will be King.

The Jews will return to the land of promise in faith. They will believe and receive their Messiah, the Lord Jesus Christ.

God has said, "I will appoint a place for My people Israel, and will plant them, that they may dwell in a place of their own and move no more; nor shall the sons of wickedness oppress them anymore" (2 Samuel 7:10). "I will bring back the captives of My people Israel; they shall build the waste cities and inhabit them; they shall plant vineyards and drink wine from them; They shall also make gardens and eat fruit from them. I will plant them in their land, And no longer shall they be pulled up from the land I have given them" (Amos 9:14–15).

The return of the Jews to their land is to bring glory to God. The twelve tribes will be identified (Matthew 19:28). A theocratic government will be established with Jesus ruling and reigning.

Scripture often speaks of the twelve tribes of Israel. Ten were lost in the Assyrian captivity of 722 BC, but God knows who they are. In the Golden Age, He will identify them by their family name (Revelation 7:1–10). Maybe DNA testing will be used to determine the tribe for each Jew. Maybe supernaturally, God will reveal it. We don't know how it's going to happen, but we know what the Bible says. The land will be divided and given to each tribe. Ezekiel tells each tribe's possessions and what section of land they will receive during the millennial reign of Christ.

Right now, Israel is a nation in unbelief, but the gathering of the Jews is not finished. Continually, there are Jews moving back to the land of promise.

Get on any flight from New York to Israel, and you will find passengers who are practicing Orthodox Jews. They're going back to Israel without any faith in Jesus Christ, but one day they will look upon Him whom they have pierced and will receive Him as their Messiah.

The Golden Age of a thousand years with Jesus as King will be a time of great jubilation. The earth will return to the beauty it had before Adam ate the forbidden fruit, was cast out of Eden, and plunged the whole creation into the curse we live under today.

All creation is looking for redemption. The apostle Paul said, "I consider that the sufferings of this present time are not worthy to be compared with the glory which shall be revealed in us. For the earnest expectation of the creation eagerly waits for the revealing of the sons of God. For the creation was subjected to futility, not willingly, but because of Him who subjected it in hope; because the creation itself also will be delivered from the bondage of corruption into the glorious liberty of the children of God" (Romans 8:18–21).

Ecological extremists groups may be well intentioned. We're commissioned by God to be good stewards of our environment. However, we're not to worship our environment or place animals or plants above the advancement of the kingdom of God. We're to subdue the earth for God's glory and humankind's good.

The clock is winding down on this sin-cursed world. When Jesus comes, He will turn back the clock to the beautiful state it was in the beginning. It will be a glorious, wondrous time. Even the animals will be at peace. "The wolf also shall dwell with the lamb, the leopard shall lie down with the young goat, the calf and the young lion and the fatling together; and a little child shall lead them. The cow and the bear shall graze; their young ones shall lie down together; and the lion shall eat straw like the ox. The nursing child shall play by the cobra's hole, and the weaned child shall put his hand in the viper's den. They shall not hurt nor destroy in all My holy mountain, for the earth shall be full of the knowledge of the LORD as the waters cover the sea. And in that day there shall be a Root of Jesse, Who shall stand as a banner to the people; for the Gentiles shall seek Him, and His resting place shall be glorious" (Isaiah 11:6–10).

Did you ever wonder why God created mosquitos? In the beginning, they had to have had a positive purpose. Somehow they got messed up just like we did. I hate snakes. They remind me of the old serpent, the Devil. But snakes did not always have a bad reputation. It wasn't always a creature to be feared, and such days will come again in the millennium. Ferocious animals will no longer attack the defenseless. It will be a time of unprecedented peace, unknown since the day Adam sinned.

The Golden Age will bring back beauty like we had in the garden of Eden. "For the LORD will comfort Zion, He will comfort all her waste places; He will make her wilderness like Eden, and her desert like the garden of the LORD; Joy and gladness will be found in it, thanksgiving and the voice of melody" (Isaiah 51:3). Crops will grow so rapidly, as soon as one is harvested, another one will be planted. 'Behold, the days are coming,' says the LORD, 'When the plowman shall overtake the reaper, and the treader of grapes him who sows seed; the mountains shall drip with sweet wine, and all the hills shall flow with it'" (Amos 9:13).

The Dead Sea will come alive with an abundance of fish. "It shall be that every living thing that moves, wherever the rivers go, will live. There will be a very great multitude of fish, because these waters go there; for they will be healed, and everything will live wherever the river goes. It shall be that fishermen will stand by it from En Gedi to En Eglaim; they will be places for spreading their nets. Their fish will be of the same kinds as the fish of the Great Sea, exceedingly many" (Ezekiel 47:9–10).

The millennium will be a wonderful and glorious time for the reclamation of productivity in the plant kingdom. We won't have to be concerned about getting enough rain. We won't have to practice crop rotation or use chemicals to reap a great harvest. During the Golden Age, there will be four growing seasons, an incredible and glorious time.

Longevity will be restored to human life. Resurrected and raptured believers will have glorified bodies like Jesus. Some people will be born and enter the millennium in physical bodies. God says, "I will rejoice in Jerusalem, and joy in My people; the voice of weeping shall no longer be heard in her, nor the voice of crying. No more shall an infant from there live but a few days, nor an old man who has not fulfilled his days; for the child shall die one hundred years old, but the sinner being one hundred years old shall be accursed" (Isaiah 65:19–20).

This is the only time the Bible mentions an age of accountability. Because Jesus went to the temple at age twelve, some think this is the age of accountability. Actually, there is a moment of God consciousness, a moment of moral accountability to God that happens in everyone during normal mental development. This could happen at any time, at age four or fourteen. If the mentally challenged never reach that place of moral responsibility, they will be safe, destined for Heaven and the Golden age.

In the millennium, a baby will be a hundred years old before reaching the age of accountability, but the sinner *being* one hundred years old shall be accursed. A person becomes accountable and responsible to God at a hundred years of age.

Let's read more about the conditions during the Golden Age: God says, "They shall build houses and inhabit them; they shall plant vineyards and eat their fruit. They shall not build and another inhabit; they shall not plant and another eat; For as the days of a tree, so shall be the days of My people, and My elect shall long enjoy the work of their hands. They shall not labor in vain, nor bring forth children for trouble; for they shall be the descendants of the blessed of the LORD, And their offspring with them. It shall come to pass that before they call, I will answer; and while they are still speaking, I will hear. The wolf and the lamb shall feed together, the lion shall eat straw like the ox, and dust shall be the serpent's food. They shall not hurt nor destroy in all My holy mountain" (Isaiah 65:21–25).

None of this has happened yet, but it *will* happen. The longevity in human life will return. Prior to the Great Flood, people lived hundreds of years before dying. You may ask, "How did these people live so long, like Methuselah who lived to be 969 years old?"

The atmosphere of the earth was different in those days, when there was no rain, but a mist came up from the ground (Genesis 2:6). The sun's rays were filtered. Physical bodies lived as long as trees, even a thousand years. Perhaps the longevity of human life will be expanded to that point once again.

For the first time on this earth, there will be peace. Everyone desires peace. The United Nations keeps failing in its effort to bring peace between nations. There will be no peace until Jesus Christ rules and reigns from Jerusalem. Then there will be joy on earth. People will

For the first time on this earth, there will be peace.

"beat their swords into plowshares, and their spears into pruning hooks; nation shall not lift up sword against nation, neither shall they learn war any more" (Micah 4:3). Jesus will rule with a rod of iron. If anyone gets out of line, He will straighten them out. There will be no need for the weapons of war.

In the Golden Age, a new temple will be constructed for worldwide worship in Jerusalem (Zechariah 14:16). Solomon built the first temple. Zerrubbabel built the second. A third will be built during the tribulation. After that, we have a millennial temple where sacrifices will not be for absolving sin, but there will be a memorial similar to the Lord's Supper. We'll be remembering what Christ has done for us, thanking Him for His blood, shed for the remission of our sins.

If you don't know Jesus as your Lord and Savior, now would

be a good time for you to open your heart to Him. If you don't make that choice now, you could be left behind without hope. When people die or when Jesus comes to take His saints to Heaven, there will be no second chance for the sinner.

You don't want to be left among those who believe a lie during the tribulation, receiving the mark of the beast, either killed or judged at the end. You will be cast away from God, with Jesus saying, "Depart from Me for I never knew you."

You can be forgiven. God loves you. He wants you to spend an eternity with Him and enjoy all the treasures of the millennium with Jesus. Praying a prayer doesn't save you, but if you will ask the Lord to come into your life, He will do it. "Whoever calls on the name of the LORD shall be saved" (Romans 10:13). If you haven't done that before, do it now.

Right where you are, you can call upon the name of the Lord. Sincerely from your heart, pray words like this: "Dear God, I know I'm a sinner. But thank you, Jesus, for dying on the cross and shedding your blood for my sin. Jesus, I invite you into my heart to be my Lord. I want to live for you. Help me do it. You said you would forgive me, and I take you at your Word. Thank you, Jesus, for giving me a home in Heaven."

As Christians, we can eagerly anticipate the coming of the Lord. As we yield to Him, He will purify our hearts and keep us clean. Whatever struggles we endure are just for a moment, for we will soon see Jesus. We will live and not die. As Jesus said, "Whoever lives and believes in Me shall never die" (John 11:26).

Every believer will soon see Jesus, whether it's through the veil of death or the parting of the clouds when He comes to take us to Heaven.

We will be with Jesus forever, in the rapture, the Golden Age, and all eternity. In that, we should leap for joy.

The Marriage Supper of the Lamb

The Marriage of the Lamb is the ceremony uniting the Lord Jesus with His bride.

> "And I heard, as it were, the voice of a great multitude, as the sound of many waters and as the sound of mighty thunderings, saying, 'Alleluia! For the Lord God Omnipotent reigns! Let us be glad and rejoice and give Him glory, for the marriage of the Lamb has come, and His wife has made herself ready. And to her it was granted to be arrayed in fine linen, clean and bright, for the fine linen is the righteous acts of the saints.' Then he said to me, 'Write: "Blessed are those who are called to the marriage supper of the Lamb!"' And he said to me, 'These are the true sayings of God.'" (Revelation 19:6–9)

Because of the setting, we can be fairly confident that the ceremony will take place in Heaven after the believers appear before the Judgment Seat of Christ and before Jesus returns to rule and reign on earth for a thousand years.

The identity of the bride is of interest. Some say it might be Israel. The Scriptures plainly show that Israel is married to the

Father. "For your Maker is your husband, The LORD of hosts is His name; and your Redeemer is the Holy One of Israel; He is called the God of the whole earth" (Isaiah 54:5). God said to Israel, "I will betroth you to Me forever; yes, I will betroth you to Me in righteousness and justice, in lovingkindness and mercy; I will betroth you to Me in faithfulness, and you shall know the LORD" (Hosea 2:19–20).

The apostle Paul uses the analogy of the church as the bride of Christ. "The husband is head of the wife, as also Christ is head of the church; and He is the Savior of the body. Therefore, just as the church is subject to Christ, so let the wives be to their own husbands in everything. Husbands, love your wives, just as Christ also loved the church and gave Himself for her, that He might sanctify and cleanse her with the washing of water by the word, that He might present her to Himself a glorious church, not having spot or wrinkle or any such thing, but that she should be holy and without blemish. So husbands ought to love their own wives as their own bodies; he who loves his wife loves himself. For no one ever hated his own flesh, but nourishes and cherishes it, just as the Lord does the church. For we are members of His body, of His flesh and of His bones. For this reason a man shall leave his father and mother and be joined to his wife, and the two shall become one flesh. This is a great mystery, but I speak concerning Christ and the church" (Ephesians 5:23–32).

The church is described as those who are born again (Hebrews 12:23). One interpretation is that all the redeemed comprise the bride of Christ. However, the church is also recognized as a local assembly of baptized believers in covenant with one another to carry out the Great Commission.

John the Baptist pointed out that he was not part of the bride (John 3:29). He was either an Old Testament saint or someone who bridged the two eras. Regardless, we know that John the Baptist was saved, yet not in the bride.

There are two points of interest in the description of the bride. She is said to "have made herself ready," and she was clothed in the "fine linen of the righteous acts of the saints." Lost people cannot make themselves ready for redemption. This is a work of grace.

It is all about who will be sitting at the head of the table.

Secondly, every believer has the imputed righteousness of Christ that clothes us before God. However, this wedding gown is a fabric of righteous acts.

One view is that being in the bride is a benefit of salvation. Another view is that being in the bride is a reward of being a faithful part of the church. The latter would explain guests, friends, and servants being at the marriage.

Following the marriage, there will be a supper. Much speculation can be raised about what will be served at the meal. Jesus said He would not drink of the fruit of the vine until His kingdom was established (Matthew 26:29). The supper might be the moment when Jesus drinks the "pure blood of the grape" again. It will be all right with me if there is filet mignon and chocolate cake. I don't think it really matters what is on the menu. It is all about who will be sitting at the head of the table.

In ancient wedding ceremonies a marriage supper could last a week. This would correspond with the week of years making up the tribulation period on earth. The supper could be directly after the Judgment Seat continuing to the end of the tribulation.

This would be quite a banquet!

Appendix

Revelation Timeline

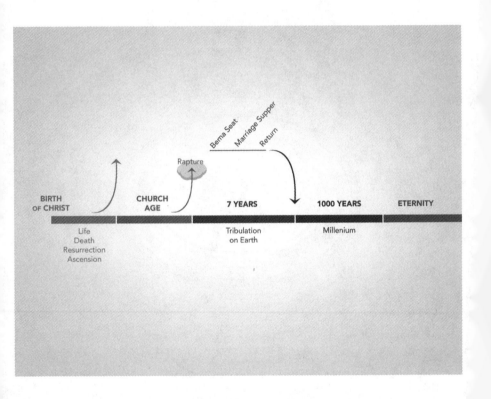

Revelation Chart

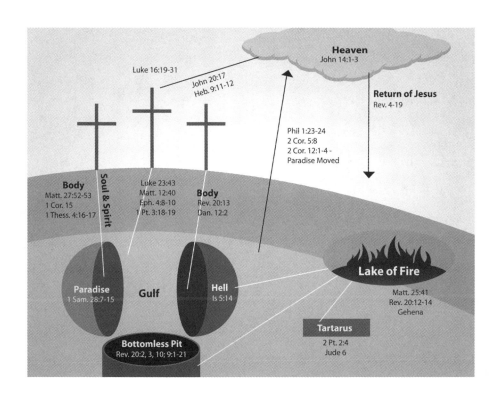

About the Author

Jim Richards was saved and answered the call to preach at age seventeen. He pastored for over twenty years, later serving as Director of Missions in Bentonville, Arkansas. He has traveled and ministered in all 50 states and 19 countries. He has preached at seminary chapel services, pastors' conferences, state conventions, and the annual meeting of the Southern Baptist Convention. Dr. Richards has served the SBC on various committees and boards, including being elected First Vice President of the Southern Baptist Convention.

Dr. Richards' education includes two undergraduate degrees, a Master of Divinity from New Orleans Baptist Theological Seminary, and a Doctor of Ministry from Mid-America Baptist Theological Seminary in Memphis. He is a Distinguished Alumnus of both seminaries. The Criswell College in Dallas awarded Dr. Richards the Doctor of Divinity in 2013.

He has authored the book, *Embracing the Ends of the Earth*, and has been a contributing author in *The Mission of Today's Church* and *Messages for the Journey.* He writes a regular column in the *TEXAN* newsmagazine.

When the Southern Baptists of Texas Convention was formed in November of 1998, Dr. Richards became the first Executive Director. The SBTC has experienced phenomenal growth both numerically and financially.

Dr. Richards and his wife, June, have three children and three grandchildren.

Connect with Dr. Richards

Twitter: @richardsjim
Facebook: https://www.facebook.com/jim.richards.733

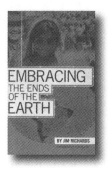

Embracing the Ends of the Earth, by Dr. Jim Richards

- Foreword by Dr. Tom Elliff, President of the International Mission Board

"When my friend Jim Richards writes in this book of the world's unengaged and unreached people groups, he does so with a passionate compulsion to see the church embrace the ends of the earth. And, as Jim states so succinctly, the ends of the earth may start in your own home, just outside your front door…or in the neighborhood diner.

As you turn the pages of this book, your heart will be stirred and your vision challenged to look on fields that are ripe unto harvest. Step by step, Jim will take you to a vantage point from which you can see the ends of the earth and show you how you can reach out with arms of love and compassion, along with a clear presentation of the gospel.

But this book is more than just another 'how-to' manual. In the process of reading about the urgency with which today's church should approach the Great Commission, you will discover plenty of practical application. After all, passion without practical application is like cheerleading without a game."

It's a God Thing, by Charles L. Roesel

- Foreword by Samuel Smith and Tim Mimms

He who has two tunics, let him give to him who has none; and he who has food, let him do likewise (Luke 3:11 NKJV).

A bold leader decided to follow Jesus' teachings, resulting in a powerful ministry that has every member in his congregation serving the poor, the downcast, and the naked. Through this obedience to Scripture, his church grew from a small fifty-member congregation to a thriving, life-filled body of Christ-followers that is active in an astounding seventy ministries today.

Learn how your church can follow Jesus today, no matter your budget or how stale your current ministry "programs," and in spite of opposition. Dr. Roesel overcame the overwhelming odds and proved that Jesus' teachings are still valid today.

In this book:

- Dr. Roesel's ministry – an incredible testimony of Ministry Evangelism
- Importance of discipleship – Jesus knew how to build a good foundation
- Leadership first – leaders must be pioneers, examples, and overcomers
- Money matters – how to avoid letting finances trip you up
- Getting started – ministry ideas that take off

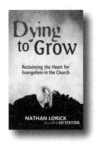

Dying to Grow, by Nathan Lorick

- Foreword by Ed Stetzer

Never before have we seen the church degenerate at such a rapid pace. This is largely due to the church pursuing congregational growth instead of kingdom growth. The church is dying because our growth isn't based on strategies to reach the lost with the gospel. The time to change is now, we can't wait any longer. People's eternities are at stake.

What is your church's priority? Are you more concerned with filling your building or furthering the Kingdom? This book will challenge you to evaluate just how important gospel-based evangelism is to you and your church, and call on you to restore an intentional evangelism strategy within the body. Hell will tremble when churches once again make evangelism the central theme of their strategy.

jubilee
B I B L E 2000

Hear what God is saying through this original translation

ANEKO Press